Editor
Janet Cain

Editorial Project Manager
Ina Massler Levin, M.A.

Editor-in-Chief
Sharon Coan, M.S. Ed.

Illustrator
Ben De Soto

Cover Artist
Jessica Orlando

Art Coordinator
Denice Adorno

Art Director
Richard D'Sa

Imaging
Alfred Lau
James Edward Grace

Product Manager
Phil Garcia

Publishers
Rachelle Cracchiolo, M.S. Ed.
Mary Dupuy Smith, M.S. Ed.

Descriptive Writing

Grades 3-5

Author

Kimberly A. Williams

Teacher Created Materials, Inc.
6421 Industry Way
Westminster, CA 92683
www.teachercreated.com

ISBN-1-57690-991-3

©2000 Teacher Created Materials, Inc.
Reprinted, 2003
Made in U.S.A.

Table of Contents

How to Use This Book

"The difference between the right word and the almost right word is the difference between lightning and the lightning bug." American author Mark Twain has spoken the truth about descriptive writing. This resource book helps you teach students that they can enhance their writing skills by choosing the right words. Students learn and apply precise word choices, sophisticated sentence structures, and effective writing techniques in seventeen skill-building lessons and sixteen writing assignments.

Following some introductory material to help students generate ideas and organize their thoughts, *Descriptive Writing: Grades 3–5* is divided into two main sections — skill-building lessons and writing assignments.

The skill-building section contains a teaching guide, student resource sheet, and student practice sheets for each skill that students will learn. The teaching guide is designed to assist you with the presentation of the skill. An activity for applying the skill, which could be used as a formative or summative assessment, is described. A student resource sheet explains each skill for students, telling what the skill is, why it is needed, when it is used, and how it is used. Examples that show how the skill is applied in writing situations are provided for student reference. Several student practice sheets are included to help students acquire mastery of the skill and apply it to their writing.

Sixteen different descriptive writing assignments are detailed in the second section. Each assignment contains a prompt that defines the assignment, revising and proofreading checklists, publishing and technology options, home-school connections, and a student sample of a completed assignment. Assessment rubrics that connect the skills with the writing assignments are provided. The criteria for excellent, satisfactory, and unsatisfactory writing are listed on the rubrics. After reading a student response, teachers can check off the statements that most apply to the piece of writing. A simple method for determining a grade is to determine which category has the most checks. For example, if most of a student's writing falls in the excellent criteria, the student would receive a top grade. If the writing is split between the excellent and satisfactory categories, the student would receive a grade in between the two, such as a *B*. Teachers can adapt the rubric checklist to meet the individual needs of their students and grading system.

Students of all ability levels can strengthen their ability to write by incorporating recently acquired skills into their writing assignments. By using this resource book, students will become more proficient and sophisticated descriptive writers.

Standards for Writing
Grades 3–5

Accompanying the major activities of this book will be references to the basic standards and benchmarks for writing that will be met by successful performance of the activities. Each specific standard and benchmark will be referred to by the appropriate letter and number from the following collection. For example, a basic standard and benchmark identified as **1A** would be as follows:

Standard 1: Demonstrates competence in the general skills and strategies of the writing process

Benchmark A: Prewriting: Uses prewriting strategies to plan written work (e.g., uses graphic organizers, story maps, and webs; groups related ideas; takes notes; brainstorms ideas)

A basic standard and benchmark identified as **4B** would be as follows:

Standard 4: Gathers and uses information for research purposes

Benchmark B: Uses encyclopedias to gather information for research topics

Clearly, some activities will address more than one standard. Moreover, since there is a rich supply of activities included in this book, some will overlap in the skills they address; and some, of course, will not address every single benchmark within a given standard. Therefore, when you see these standards referenced in the activities, refer to this section for complete descriptions.

Although virtually every state has published its own standards and every subject area maintains its own lists, there is surprising commonality among these various sources. For the purposes of this book, we have elected to use the collection of standards synthesized by John S. Kendall and Robert J. Marzano in their book *Content Knowledge: A Compendium of Standards and Benchmarks for K–12 Education* (Second Edition, 1997) as illustrative of what students at various grade levels should know and be able to do. The book is published jointly by McREL (Mid-continent Regional Educational Laboratory, Inc.) and ASCD (Association for Supervision and Curriculum Development). (Used by permission of McREL.)

Language Arts Standards

1. Demonstrates competence in the general skills and strategies of the writing process

2. Demonstrates competence in the stylistic and rhetorical aspects of writing

3. Uses grammatical and mechanical conventions in written compositions

4. Gathers and uses information for research purposes

Standards for Writing
Grades 3–5 *(cont.)*

Level II (Grades 3–5)

1. Demonstrates competence in the general skills and strategies of the writing process

- **A. Prewriting:** Uses prewriting strategies to plan written work (e.g., uses graphic organizers, story maps, and webs; group-related ideas; takes notes; brainstorms ideas)

- **B. Drafting and Revising:** Uses strategies to draft and revise written work (e.g., elaborates on a central idea; writes with attention to voice, audience, word choice, tone, and imagery; uses paragraphs to develop separate ideas)

- **C. Editing and Publishing:** Uses strategies to edit and publish written work (e.g., edits for grammar, punctuation, capitalization, and spelling at a developmentally appropriate level; considers page format [paragraphs, margins, indentations, titles]; selects presentation format; incorporates photos, illustrations, charts, and graphs)

- **D.** Evaluates own and others' writing (e.g., identifies the best features of a piece of writing, determines how own writing achieves its purposes, asks for feedback, responds to classmates' writing)

- **E.** Writes stories or essays that show awareness of intended audience

- **F.** Writes stories or essays that convey an intended purpose (e.g., to record ideas, to describe, to explain)

- **G.** Writes expository compositions (e.g., identifies and stays on the topic; develops the topic with simple facts, details, examples, and explanations; excludes extraneous and inappropriate information)

- **H.** Writes narrative accounts (e.g., engages the reader by establishing a context and otherwise creates an organizational structure that balances and unifies all narrative aspects of the story; uses sensory details and concrete language to develop plot and character; uses a range of strategies such as dialogue and tension or suspense)

- **I.** Writes autobiographical compositions (e.g., provides a context within which the incident occurs, uses simple narrative strategies, provides some insight into why this incident is memorable)

- **J.** Writes expressive compositions (e.g., expresses ideas, reflections, and observations; uses an individual, authentic voice; uses narrative strategies, relevant details, and ideas that enable the reader to imagine the world of the event or experience)

- **K.** Writes in response to literature (e.g., advances judgements; supports judgements with references to the text, other works, other authors, nonprint media, and personal knowledge)

- **L.** Writes personal letters (e.g., includes the date, address, greeting, and closing; addresses envelopes)

Standards for Writing
Grades 3–5 *(cont.)*

Level II (cont.)

2. Demonstrates competence in the stylistic and rhetorical aspects of writing

  A. Uses descriptive language that clarifies and enhances ideas (e.g., describes familiar people, places, or objects)

  B. Uses paragraph form in writing (e.g., indents the first word of a paragraph, uses topic sentences, recognizes a paragraph as a group of sentences about one main idea, writes several related paragraphs)

  C. Uses a variety of sentence structures

3. Uses grammatical and mechanical conventions in written compositions

  A. Writes in cursive

  B. Uses exclamatory and imperative sentences in written compositions

  C. Uses pronouns in written compositions (e.g., substitutes pronouns for nouns)

  D. Uses nouns in written compositions (e.g., uses plural and singular naming words; forms regular and irregular plurals of nouns; uses common and proper nouns; uses nouns as subjects)

  E. Uses verbs in written compositions (e.g., uses a wide variety of action verbs, past and present verb tenses, simple tenses, forms of regular verbs, verbs that agree with the subject)

  F. Uses adjectives in written compositions (e.g., indefinite, numerical, predicate adjectives)

  G. Uses adverbs in written compositions (e.g., to make comparisons)

  H. Uses coordinating conjunctions in written compositions (e.g., links ideas using connecting words)

  I. Uses negatives in written compositions (e.g., avoids double negatives)

  J. Uses conventions of spelling in written compositions (e.g., spells high frequency, commonly misspelled words from appropriate grade-level list; uses a dictionary and other resources to spell words; uses initial consonant substitution to spell related words; uses vowel combinations for correct spelling)

  K. Uses conventions of capitalization in written compositions (e.g., titles of people; proper nouns [names of towns, cities, counties, and states; days of the week; months of the year; names of streets; names of countries; holidays]; first word of direct quotations; heading, salutation, and closing of a letter)

  L. Uses conventions of punctuation in written compositions (e.g., uses periods after imperative sentences and in initials, abbreviations, and titles before names; uses commas in dates and addresses and after greetings and closings in a letter; uses apostrophes in contractions and possessive nouns; uses quotation marks around titles and with direct quotations; uses a colon between hours and minutes)

Standards for Writing
Grades 3–5 *(cont.)*

Level II (cont.)

> **4. Gathers and uses information for research purposes**

    A. Uses a variety of strategies to identify topics to investigate (e.g., brainstorms, lists questions, uses idea webs)

    B. Uses encyclopedias to gather information for research topics

    C. Uses dictionaries to gather information for research topics

    D. Uses key words, indexes, cross-references, and letters on volumes to find information for research topics

    E. Uses multiple representations of information (e.g., maps, charts, photos) to find information for research topics

    F. Uses graphic organizers (e.g., notes, charts, graphs) to gather and record information for research topics

    G. Compiles information into written reports or summaries

Generating Ideas for Writing

Picture File: Create a picture file that students can use as a stimulus for writing. Collect pictures from calendars, magazines, newspapers, or even personal photos that might be intriguing or spark an idea in a student's mind. You may wish to mount the pictures on construction paper or poster board and laminate them for durability. Keep the pictures in a box in your classroom for easy access. You may even wish to have students create a personal picture file as a long-term homework assignment.

Idea Center: Create an area of your classroom that can be designated as the Idea Center. Allow students to visit this center when they need ideas for writing. Stock it with all kinds of material that may spark students' creativity: baby naming books, encyclopedias, rhyming dictionaries, newspapers, magazines, maps, atlases, artwork, cassette tapes and headphones, advertisements, fliers, phone books, postcards, etc. The possibilities are endless. You never know where a student might get a good idea for writing.

Prop Box: Obtain a fairly large box with a lid, such as those used to hold reams of copier paper. Cover the box and lid with contact paper to give it an attractive appearance. Fill the box with various items: a running shoe, sunglasses, a shawl, a beaded purse, an empty stick of deodorant, an umbrella, an empty bottle of sunscreen, a box of tissues, a belt—the crazier, the better. Allow each student to pick an item from the box and use that as the subject for a writing assignment.

Word Wheels: Obtain several cardboard pizza wheels from a local pizza store or cut large circles out of cardboard. Use a marker to divide the wheels into eight "slices." On one wheel, write a different noun in each of the "slices." On another wheel, write a different verb in each of the "slices." Make two more wheels, writing different adjectives and adverbs on them. Cut out a cardboard arrow for each wheel. Punch a hole in the center of the arrows and the center of the wheels. Then use a metal brad to connect an arrow to the center of each wheel. Students can spin the arrows on each wheel and challenge themselves to use the selected words in a writing assignment.

Word Wall: Design a bulletin board to help students select precise words for their writing. Collect 26 envelopes or small boxes. Even clean French fry containers from a local fast food restaurant will work. Print a letter of the alphabet on each container. Then place several strips of paper, showing adjectives that begin with that letter of the alphabet, in each container. For example, the *A* container could have strips that say: *awesome, amazing, ailing, alone, altruistic,* and *ancient*. Students may search the containers for the right word to use when working on a writing assignment. Remind youngsters to make sure they put the strips back in the correct envelopes or boxes. This bulletin board could also be used as a vocabulary building activity by having students look up the meaning of the words in a dictionary. The title of your bulletin board could be "Around the Alphabet with Adjectives." You may wish to have students create this bulletin board as a class project in preparation for starting the unit on descriptive writing.

Sensory Center: Help students generate sensory words with first-hand experiences. Place plenty of scrap paper and pencils in the center for students to jot down sensory words as they experience them. Then make a variety of sensory boxes by placing "mystery" items in covered boxes. You should design one box for each of the five senses. In the sight box, line the box with metallic or sparkly paper. Allow students to hold the box up to their eyes and look through two holes that you have cut in the side of the box. In the smell box, soak cotton balls in perfume or vanilla extract and place them in the box. Allow students to place their noses near the hole that you have cut in the box and take a sniff. In the sound box, place lots of marbles. Then instruct students to roll or shake the box. In the touch box, line the bottom of a long box with several different textured materials (burlap, fake fur, cellophane, bubble wrap, etc.). Invite students to reach their fingers into sets of holes that you have cut in the box. Tell them to feel the different materials inside. In the taste box, place small resealable plastic bags with a small amount of food, such as raisins or chocolate chips, for students to taste. Remind students to conduct only one taste test.

Warning: Be sure to ask parents if their children have any food allergies or dietary restrictions before allowing students to conduct this taste test.

Nouns

Teaching Guide

Goal: The students will recognize nouns and generate specific nouns to enhance their descriptive writing.

Introducing the Skill

Preparation: Reproduce the Student Resource Sheet (page 10) for students and make a copy for yourself to use as a teaching reference.

Directions: Distribute the Student Resource Sheet to students. Tell students WHAT skill they will be learning. Explain WHY writers use this skill and WHY it will make your students' writing better. Show several examples of WHEN this skill is used. Teach students HOW to use this skill.

Practicing the Skill

Preparation: Reproduce the Student Practice Sheets (pages 11 and 12) for students.

Directions: Assign the practice sheets to students according to their needs and abilities. You may wish to have students work on these sheets in one or more of the following ways: as a whole-class activity, with a partner, in small groups, or independently. As an alternative, you may prefer to use one or both sheets as homework assignments. Provide feedback to students to ensure mastery of the skill.

Applying the Skill

Preparation: None

Directions: Play a classroom version of the game "I Spy." Select a person, place, or thing in the classroom. Do not tell students the noun you have selected. Describe the noun by saying, for example, "I spy something that is oval-shaped, made of metal, and eats pencils." *(a pencil sharpener)* Have students guess the noun you are describing. The first student to correctly guess the noun gets a chance to locate the next noun and describe it for the class. Continue in this manner until all students have had a chance to describe a noun.

Student Resource Sheet

What: Good writers use nouns in their writing. A noun is a word that names a person, place, or thing.

Why: Nouns are usually the subjects of sentences. They are one of the basic parts of every sentence. Nouns help the reader make sense of the writing.

When: At least one noun needs to be used in each sentence. Many sentences have more than one noun.

How: Nouns are easy to use. A very simple sentence could contain just a noun and a verb. For example, in the sentence "Dogs run," *dogs* is the noun.

Here are some examples of different kinds of nouns.

People	Places	Things
babysitter	Baltimore	ankle
Barbara Jordan	California	apple
brother	city	birthday
character	continent	chair
comedian	field	football
David	General Hospital	hamburger
doctor	hospital	horse
grandfather	museum	kindness
Lois	neighborhood	liberty
manager	office	money
Mr. Smith	park	mouse
Ms. Johnson	restaurant	newspaper
neighbor	stadium	radio
owner	store	roses
president	theater	silence
sister	town	table
Superman	valley	turkey
captain	yard	window

Standards and Benchmarks: 3D, 3K

Student Practice Sheet One

Determine if each of the following words is a noun. If the word is a noun, write *Yes* in the blank after the word. If it is not a noun, write *No*.

1. friend _____
2. awful _____
3. lonely _____
4. Aunt Susan _____
5. ancient _____
6. Abraham Lincoln _____
7. church _____
8. walked _____
9. game _____
10. hospital _____

11. grandmother _____
12. David _____
13. talking _____
14. London _____
15. Dr. Jones _____
16. unique _____
17. pretty _____
18. feel _____
19. really _____
20. freedom _____

Now use each of the following nouns in a sentence.

21. flowers _____
22. computer _____
23. sister _____
24. Washington, D.C. _____
25. money _____
26. graveyard _____
27. Daniel _____
28. city _____
29. patients _____
30. patience _____

Note: Fold under before reproducing.

Answer Key

1. Yes	3. No	5. No	7. Yes	9. Yes	11. Yes	13. No	15. Yes	17. No	19. No
2. No	4. Yes	6. Yes	8. No	10. Yes	12. Yes	14. Yes	16. No	18. No	20. Yes

Standards and Benchmarks: 3D, 3K

Student Practice Sheet Two

Each of the following sentences has at least one noun in it. However, the noun that is used is not very descriptive. Replace each boldfaced noun with a more specific noun. This will give the reader a clear mental picture of what the sentence is about and it will make the writing more interesting.

1. Please give me that **tool**.

   Please give me that _____ .

2. We gave Mom some **flowers** for her birthday.

   We gave Mom some _____ for her birthday.

3. I ordered a **dessert** after I ate dinner.

   I ordered a _____ after I ate dinner.

4. The thief got into the **car** and sped away.

   The thief got into the _____ and sped away.

5. The family lived in a **place** overlooking the ocean.

   The family lived in a _____ overlooking the ocean.

6. We won the **game**.

   We won the _____.

7. Watch out for that **animal**!

   Watch out for that _____!

8. The captain of the **boat** was at least 70 years old.

   The captain of the _____ was at least 70 years old.

9. Jenny hit the **ball** into the grass.

   Jenny hit the _____ into the grass.

10. Turn that **machine** off right away!

    Turn that _____ off right away!

11. The **building** was on fire.

    The _____ was on fire.

12. My **pet** is always happy to see me when I get home.

    My _____ is always happy to see me when I get home.

Verbs

Teaching Guide

Goal: The students will use action verbs to provide clarification and description in writing.

Introducing the Skill

Preparation: Reproduce the Student Resource Sheet (page 14) for students and make a copy for yourself to use as a teaching reference.

Directions: Distribute the Student Resource Sheet to students. Tell students WHAT skill they will be learning. Explain WHY writers use this skill and WHY it will make your students' writing better. Show several examples of WHEN this skill is used. Teach students HOW to use this skill.

Practicing the Skill

Preparation: Reproduce the Student Practice Sheets (pages 15 and 16) for students.

Directions: Assign the practice sheets to students according to their needs and abilities. You may wish to have students work on these sheets in one or more of the following ways: as a whole-class activity, with a partner, in small groups, or independently. As an alternative, you may prefer to use one or both sheets as homework assignments. Provide feedback to students to ensure mastery of the skill.

Applying the Skill

Preparation: Write verbs on slips of paper. You will need enough slips for each student in the class to have one. Place the slips in a container, such as a hat, bag, or small box. The following verbs work well for this activity.

skip	sing	catch	fight	sit
jump	blow	fall	write	dance
sleep	eat	shake	jog	bite
drive	hide	swim	drink	drown
cry	walk	throw	draw	paint
sniff	hit	dive	fly	type

Directions: Tell students that they are going to play a version of charades. Choose a student to select a slip of paper from the container. Instruct that student to read the word on the slip of paper to him/herself. The student should then "act out" the word for the class. The rest of the class should try to guess what word is on the slip of paper based on the action being performed. Continue with the game until all students have had a chance to act out a word.

Student Resource Sheet

What: Good writers use strong, specific verbs to describe the actions of a character (a person, animal, or thing).

Why: Strong verbs paint a more vivid picture for the reader. They describe exactly what the character is doing. Sometimes strong verbs even give clues to a character's motivation or emotions.

When: Writers use strong verbs all the time. Anytime you write a sentence, try to use a verb that is as specific and as strong as possible.

How: Think about the subject (who or what) your sentence is about. Decide what the subject of your sentence is doing. Think about why the subject is doing this action. Then choose the most specific verb to describe the action being done by your subject. You may need to consult a thesaurus or dictionary to help you select the best verb. Some verbs describe an action that is happening in the present, or now. Other verbs describe an action that has already happened, which means it has taken place in the past.

Here are some examples of verbs.

run	sing	searched	rang	helping
sit	speak	began	blew	researching
swim	shine	broke	coloring	computing
sink	try	fought	painting	calculating
drive	sew	gave	organizing	feeding
catch	lost	took	thinking	fixing
throw	fell	talked	moving	winning
eat	looked	tore	sliding	

Note: Remember, verbs show action. They must tell something the subject of your sentence can do.

Standards and Benchmarks: 3E

Student Practice Sheet One

Brainstorm a list of synonyms for the word *went* as it is used in the following sentence.

| The person **went** down the road. |

Example: *skipped*

_____ _____ _____

_____ _____ _____

_____ _____ _____

_____ _____ _____

_____ _____ _____

_____ _____ _____

_____ _____ _____

_____ _____ _____

Select five of your synonyms from above. For each word, imagine what kind of character would move that way. Why might the character be moving in that way? Review the example shown below. Then list your five synonyms under the word *skipped*. For each synonym, include a brief explanation of who would move that way and why.

Synonym	Who would move that way?	Why?
Example: *skipped*	*a little girl*	*She's excited because it's her birthday.*

Standards and Benchmarks: 3E

Student Practice Sheet Two

Read the following pairs of sentences. Place an **X** beside the sentence that is more exciting or interesting to read.

1. _____ The prisoner walked back and forth in his cell.

   _____ The prisoner paced back and forth in his cell.

2. _____ The basketball team bolted onto the court, ready to play the championship game.

   _____ The basketball team walked onto the court, ready to play the championship game.

3. _____ The happy dog raced across the grass.

   _____ The happy dog ran across the grass.

4. _____ The man gobbled his food as if he hadn't eaten in days.

   _____ The man ate his food as if he hadn't eaten in days.

Read the following sentences. Replace each verb in parentheses with a stronger, more specific action verb.

5. The children _____ into the swimming pool. (went)

6. The monkey _____ on the tree branch and _____ its banana. (sat; ate)

7. The tired man _____ to bed. (went)

8. Anthony _____ from the slide and _____ in the mud puddle at the bottom. (fell; landed)

9. The pitcher _____ the ball toward the batter. (threw)

10. The pilot _____ the airplane through the thick fog and landed it safely. (flew)

11. The cheetah _____ for food. (looked)

12. Jake's car _____ around the corner, _____ on the wet pavement, and _____ on the curb. (went; slipped; landed)

13. The chef _____ a five-course dinner, fit for a king. (made)

14. The lazy dog _____ in the warm sunshine. (slept)

15. Suddenly, the door _____ open. (came)

Adjectives
Teaching Guide

Goal: The students will recognize adjectives and generate adjectives to enhance their descriptive writing.

Introducing the Skill

Preparation: Reproduce the Student Resource Sheet (page 18) for students and make a copy for yourself to use as a teaching reference.

Directions: Distribute the Student Resource Sheet to students. Tell students WHAT skill they will be learning. Explain WHY writers use this skill and WHY it will make your students' writing better. Show several examples of WHEN this skill is used. Teach students HOW to use this skill.

Practicing the Skill

Preparation: Reproduce the Student Practice Sheets (pages 19 and 20) for students.

Directions: Discuss what adjectives are. Explain that adjectives can have positive or negative connotations. Then assign the practice sheets to students according to their needs and abilities. You may wish to have students work on these sheets in one or more of the following ways: as a whole-class activity, with a partner, in small groups, or independently. As an alternative, you may prefer to use one or both sheets as homework assignments. Provide feedback to students to ensure mastery of the skill.

Applying the Skill

Preparation: None

Directions: Play a version of "I'm going on a trip…" with students. Beginning with the letter *A*, go around the room and have each student say what she/he would like to take on the trip. The item should be an adjective and a noun that begin with the same letter. For example, you could start with "I'm going on a trip, and I'm planning to take an **attractive alien**." The first student should repeat what you are taking and add an item (adjective + noun) that starts with the letter *B*. The game continues in this manner until you reach the end of the alphabet. If you have more than 26 students, start back at the beginning of the alphabet and continue until every student has had an opportunity to participate. You may wish to record on chart paper or a chalkboard what each person is taking to review the adjectives after the activity.

Student Resource Sheet

What: Good writers use many adjectives in their writing to add interest and sophistication to their writing. An adjective is a word that describes a noun (person, place, or thing). Adjectives generally tell which one, what kind, how many, or how much.

Why: Adjectives add description to writing. They give the reader more information about the subject and help paint a clearer picture in the reader's mind. Adjectives help the writer to be precise, as well as interesting.

When: Adjectives are generally used before the noun that they describe.

How: Using adjectives is easy. Simply think of your subject and put one or more describing words before it.

Here are some examples:

- The following adjectives tell **which one:**

  new puppy
  blue shoe
  swollen knee
  biggest ball

- The following adjectives tell **what kind:**

  sunny day
  loud thunderstorm
  famous actor
  chocolate cake

- The following adjectives tell **how many:**

  eight legs
  sixteen cupcakes
  two gallons
  nine miles

- The following adjectives tell **how much:**

  several books
  few raisins
  many shoes
  some information

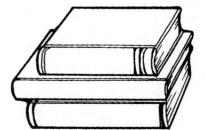

Standards and Benchmarks: 2A, 3F

Student Practice Sheet One

Add an adjective before each noun listed below to tell which one, what kind, how many, or how much.

1. _____ highway

2. _____ dinner

3. _____ car

4. _____ oranges

5. _____ children

6. _____ movie

7. _____ trees

8. _____ cowboy

9. _____ celebration

10. _____ city

Now use the same adjectives and nouns from the above activity and create an interesting sentence for each pair of words. For example, if you wrote *narrow highway* above, your sentence could be *I cautiously drove my eighteen-wheeler down the narrow highway.*

11. _____

12. _____

13. _____

14. _____

15. _____

16. _____

17. _____

18. _____

19. _____

20. _____

Standards and Benchmarks: 2A, 3F

Student Practice Sheet Two

Complete the following chart by writing adjectives. Under each heading (Eyes, Nose, Hair, Lips, Skin), brainstorm a list of adjectives that could be used to describe that part of a person. Look at the examples provided. The adjectives may have positive or negative connotations. Think of as many different adjectives as you can.

Eyes	Nose	Hair	Lips	Skin
sparkling	crooked	curly	thin	pale

Adverbs

Teaching Guide

Goal: The students will use adverbs to expand and clarify their writing.

Introducing the Skill

Preparation: Reproduce the Student Resource Sheet (page 22) for students and make a copy for yourself to use as a teaching reference.

Directions: Distribute the Student Resource Sheet to students. Tell students WHAT skill they will be learning. Explain WHY writers use this skill and WHY it will make your students' writing better. Show several examples of WHEN this skill is used. Teach students HOW to use this skill.

Practicing the Skill

Preparation: Reproduce the Student Practice Sheets (pages 23 and 24) for students.

Directions: Assign the practice sheets to students according to their needs and abilities. You may wish to have students work on these sheets in one or more of the following ways: as a whole-class activity, with a partner, in small groups, or independently. As an alternative, you may prefer to use one or both sheets as homework assignments. Provide feedback to students to ensure mastery of the skill.

Applying the Skill

Preparation: Write adverbs that tell *how* on slips of paper. You will need enough slips for each student in the class to have one. Place the slips in a container, such as a hat, bag, or small box. The following adverbs work well for this activity.

softly	loudly	gently	playfully	hesitantly	sadly
carefully	slowly	sharply	lazily	suddenly	happily
quickly	foolishly	sweetly	nervously	hurriedly	angrily

Directions: Play charades with students. Choose a student to select a slip of paper from the container. Instruct that student to read the word on the slip of paper to him/herself. The student should then "act out" the word for the class. The rest of the class should try to guess what word is on the slip of paper based on the action being performed. Continue with the game until all students have had a chance to act out a word.

Student Resource Sheet

What: Good writers use adverbs to tell *when, how, where,* or *how often* the subject of a sentence performs an action. An adverb is a word that describes a verb.

Why: Good writers use adverbs to make their writing clearer and more specific.

When: Adverbs are used when a writer wants to give more information about a subject's actions. If the writer wants to tell *when, how, where,* or *how often* the subject performs an action, an adverb is used.

How: Most adverbs are placed after verbs. However, sometimes they are placed before verbs.

- Here are some examples of adverbs that are placed after verbs.

  1. We worked.

     We worked **yesterday**. (tells *when*)

  2. The children spoke.

     The children spoke **softly**. (tells *how*)

  3. The ball rolled.

     The ball rolled **away**. (tells *where*)

  4. It rained.

     It rained **twice**. (tells *how often*)

- Here are some examples of adverbs that are placed before verbs.

  1. I read before going to sleep.

     I **often** read before going to sleep. (tells *how often*)

  2. Dad removed the splinter from my finger.

     Dad **carefully** removed the splinter from my finger. (tells *how*)

  3. Natalie shouted, "Come here!"

     Natalie **quickly** shouted, "Come here!" (tells *how*)

Standards and Benchmarks: 3G

Student Practice Sheet One

An adverb is a word that describes a verb. Adverbs usually tell *when, how, where,* or *how often.*

Read the following sentences. Circle the verbs. Underline the adverbs. On the line following each sentence, write whether the adverb in that sentence tells *when, how, where,* or *how often.*

1. Dad snores loudly. _____

2. Aunt Jenny quickly cooked dinner. _____

3. My brother watches videos daily. _____

4. Susan gently stroked the soft kitten. _____

5. The leaves blew up from the ground. _____

6. I exercised today. _____

7. The plane arrived late. _____

8. My mother plants flowers outside. _____

9. My mother plants flowers annually. _____

10. Recently, I went to a concert. _____

11. He answered the question thoughtfully. _____

12. I ate pizza for lunch today. _____

13. Yesterday, I learned how to roller blade. _____

14. Foolishly, the children went outside without their coats. _____

15. We take piano lessons weekly. _____

- -

Note: Fold under before reproducing.

Answer Key

Verbs should be circled. Adverbs should be underlined.

1. Verb: **snores**; Adverb: **loudly**—tells *how*
2. Verb: **cooked**; Adverb: **quickly**—tells *how*
3. Verb: **watches**; Adverb: **daily**—tells *how often*
4. Verb: **stroked**; Adverb: **gently**—tells *how*
5. Verb: **blew**; Adverb: **up**—tells *where*
6. Verb: **exercised**; Adverb: **today**—tells *when*
7. Verb: **arrived**; Adverb: **late**—tells *when*
8. Verb: **plants**; Adverb: **outside**—tells *where*
9. Verb: **plants**; Adverb: **annually**—tells *how often*
10. Verb: **went**; Adverb: **recently**—tells *when*
11. Verb: **answered**; Adverb: **thoughtfully**—tells *how*
12. Verb: **ate**; Adverb: **today**—tells *when*
13. Verb: **learned**; Adverb: **yesterday**—tells *when*
14. Verb: **went**; Adverb: **foolishly**—tells *how*
15. Verb: **take**; Adverb: **weekly**—tells *how often*

Standards and Benchmarks: 3G

Student Practice Sheet Two

You can have fun with adverbs by using humor when you add them to sentences. Read each sentence. Determine which adverb from the box is most appropriate to complete each sentence. Use each adverb once. With the adverbs, the sentences should be funny. The first one has been done for you.

flatly	strikingly	heavily	patiently	playfully
tiredly	dimly	rashly	sharply	listlessly
sweetly	saucily	mechanically	offhandedly	heartily

1. "Ouch! I just cut myself with this knife!" he said _____ sharply _____.

2. "This hot chocolate tastes great," she said _____.

3. "I just blew out my car tire," the man said _____.

4. "That lightning is amazing," the photographer said _____.

5. "Does anyone know how to replace a light bulb?" he asked _____.

6. "Will you be my Valentine?" he asked _____.

7. "I think I have poison ivy," she said _____.

8. "I've gained so much weight," he said _____.

9. "I forgot what I was supposed to buy at the grocery store," Dad said _____.

10. "I'm exhausted," Mom said _____.

11. "I'll never stick my hand in the lion's cage again!" he said _____.

12. "This spaghetti sauce sure is tangy," she said _____.

13. "I got the lead in the play *Romeo and Juliet*," she said _____.

14. "Who is next to see the doctor?" the nurse asked _____.

15. "I'm good at fixing cars," she said _____.

Note: Fold under before reproducing.

Answer Key

Possible answers:

1. sharply	6. heartily	11. offhandedly
2. sweetly	7. rashly	12. saucily
3. flatly	8. heavily	13. playfully
4. strikingly	9. listlessly	14. patiently
5. dimly	10. tiredly	15. mechanically

Sensory Words
Teaching Guide

Goal: The students will use sensory words to provide precision and clarification in descriptive writing.

Introducing the Skill

Preparation: Reproduce the Student Resource Sheet (page 26) for students and make a copy for yourself to use as a teaching reference.

Directions: Distribute the Student Resource Sheet to students. Tell students WHAT skill they will be learning. Explain WHY writers use this skill and WHY it will make your students' writing better. Show several examples of WHEN this skill is used. Teach students HOW to use this skill.

Practicing the Skill

Preparation: Reproduce the Student Practice Sheets (pages 27–31) for students.

Directions: Assign the practice sheets to students according to their needs and abilities. You may wish to have students work on these sheets in one or more of the following ways: as a whole-class activity, with a partner, in small groups, or independently. As an alternative, you may prefer to use one or both sheets as homework assignments. Provide feedback to students to ensure mastery of the skill.

Applying the Skill

Preparation: Reproduce the Student Worksheet (page 32) for students. Obtain a variety of magazines and sale flyers that contain advertisements. You will need enough for each student in the class to be able to look through at least one.

Directions: Distribute copies of the Student Worksheet to students. Provide each student with a magazine or flyer. Direct students to look through the magazines and flyers, paying particular attention to advertisements. Instruct students to examine the advertisements and jot down any examples of sensory words that are used to describe the products. When students have had sufficient time to gather examples, ask them to share these with the class.

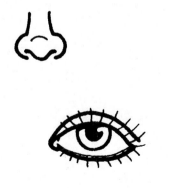

Student Resource Sheet

What: Good writers use sensory words to evoke strong images in the reader's mind.

Why: Good writers use sensory words to provide clear, concise, and precise descriptions.

When: Sensory words that appeal to all of the reader's five senses should be used throughout a piece of descriptive writing. The more descriptive the writing, the stronger the reader's sensory response will be.

How: Sensory words can be used to appeal to a reader's sense of sight, hearing, touch, smell, or taste. Any time you are describing something, you can use sensory words to make your description more vivid for the reader.

Here are some examples of different types of sensory words.

Sight Words	Sound Words	Touch Words
twinkle	clink	soft
shine	rattle	scratchy
turquoise	hum	silky
glowing	buzz	smooth
murky	moan	cold
cloudy	whistle	hard
sparkle	snort	gooey
cascade	sputter	slimy
luminous	whirl	slick
bright	wheeze	slippery
hazy	cough	leathery
glittery	bang	rough

Smell Words	Taste Words
musty	sweet
flowery	creamy
sweet	spicy
foul	salty
pungent	bitter
ripe	tangy
dank	juicy
aromatic	fruity
reeking	cheesy
odorous	sour
fragrant	buttery
perfumed	garlicky

Standards and Benchmarks: 2A, 3D, 3F

Student Practice Sheet One

List as many different shades of the following colors as possible.

Blue

Red

Yellow

Purple

Orange

Brown

Black

White

Green

Standards and Benchmarks: 2A, 3D, 3F

Student Practice Sheet Two

List some sounds that you might hear in each of the following places.

1. at a park	**2. at a playground**
3. at school dismissal	**4. at a church**
5. at a zoo	**6. at a grocery store**
7. at a dentist's office	**8. at a ballpark**
9. at a library	**10. at a police station**

Where might you hear . . .

- a piercing scream? _____
- a vicious growl? _____
- water dripping? _____
- a phone ringing? _____
- a tired yawn? _____

Standards and Benchmarks: 2A, 3D, 3F

Student Practice Sheet Three

Place a check in one or more boxes to describe the taste of each food.

	pepperoni pizza	an orange	spaghetti	cinnamon toast	a lemon	grilled cheese sandwich	caramel apple
bitter							
sweet							
spicy							
salty							
tangy							
creamy							
juicy							
fruity							
chocolatey							
sour							
burnt							
cheesy							
buttery							
greasy							
crunchy							
garlicky							
sugary							
gooey							

Standards and Benchmarks: 2A, 3D, 3F

Student Practice Sheet Four

Write a sentence that describes each item.

Describe how these items look.

1. statue _____
2. snowflake _____
3. ocean _____
4. dress _____
5. car _____

Describe how these items sound.

6. train _____
7. marching band _____
8. fireworks _____
9. thunder _____
10. car crash _____

Describe how these items feel.

11. straw _____
12. concrete _____
13. ice _____
14. blanket _____
15. dog _____

Describe how these items smell.

16. flower _____
17. cookies _____
18. dirty socks _____
19. hospital _____
20. restaurant _____

Describe how these items taste.

21. pizza _____
22. banana _____
23. milkshake _____
24. orange juice _____
25. bubble gum _____

Standards and Benchmarks: 2A, 3D, F

Student Practice Sheet Five

Pretend that you are shopping in a grocery store. Answer the following questions using words that appeal to the senses.

Here is an example: How did the boxes of cereal **look** on the shelf in the cereal aisle? *neat and organized; like soldiers lined up for duty*

1. How do the vegetables **look** in the produce department?_____

_____

2. How does the bag of frozen peas **feel** in the freezer?_____

_____

3. How do the muffins **smell** in the bakery? _____

_____

4. How does the sample of grape juice **taste** in the juice aisle? _____

_____

5. How do the cash registers **sound** when you are checking out? _____

_____

Now write a sentence to describe each item using the words that appeal to the senses that you listed above.

Here is an example: How do the boxes of cereal look in the cereal aisle? *The cereal stood neat and organized on the shelf, like soldiers lined up for duty.*

6. How do the vegetables **look** in the produce department?_____

_____

7. How does the bag of frozen peas **feel** in the freezer?_____

_____

8. How do the muffins **smell** in the bakery? _____

_____

9. How does the sample of grape juice **taste** in the juice aisle? _____

_____

10. How do the cash registers **sound** when you are checking out? _____

_____

Standards and Benchmarks: 2A, 3D, 3F

Student Worksheet

Sense-ational Advertising

Look at advertisements in a magazine or flyer. Find words in the advertisements that appeal to the senses. Use the organizer below to list these words.

👁 Sight Words 👁

👂 Sound Words 👂

✋ Touch Words ✋

👃 Smell Words 👃

👄 Taste Words 👄

Connotative Language
Teaching Guide

Goal: The students will consider the positive and negative connotations of language in order to identify and integrate persuasive techniques in descriptive writing.

Introducing the Skill

Preparation: Reproduce the Student Resource Sheet (page 34) for students and make a copy for yourself to use as a teaching reference.

Directions: Distribute the Student Resource Sheet to students. Tell students WHAT skill they will be learning. Explain WHY writers use this skill and WHY it will make your students' writing better. Show several examples of WHEN this skill is used. Teach students HOW to use this skill.

Practicing the Skill

Preparation: Reproduce the Student Practice Sheets (pages 35 and 36) for students.

Directions: Review what positive and negative connotations are. Assign the practice sheets to students according to their needs and abilities. You may wish to have students work on these sheets in one or more of the following ways: as a whole-class activity, with a partner, in small groups, or independently. As an alternative, you may prefer to use one or both sheets as homework assignments. Provide feedback to students to ensure mastery of the skill.

Applying the Skill

Preparation: Obtain a variety of toy cars, one for each pair of students.

Directions: Assign partners or allow students to choose their own. Have one youngster from each pair of students be a "buyer" and the other be a "seller." Give one toy car to each pair of students. Instruct students to pretend that the buyers are shopping for a used car and the sellers are the used car salespeople. Tell the sellers to choose words with positive connotations to describe the used car to the buyer. Have the buyers record the words with positive connotations that the seller uses to describe the car. After students have role-played the scenario, ask the buyers to share the words the sellers used to describe the cars in a positive manner. Encourage them to tell which words were most effective and why. Then allow students to switch roles, and repeat the activity.

Student Resource Sheet

What: Good writers are aware of the positive and negative connotations of words. Connotation means the feeling or emotions created by a word. For example, the two words *aroma* and *stench* both refer to smells. *Aroma* has a positive connotation. You usually hear that word used to describe fragrant flowers, perfume, or the smell of something delicious cooking. *Stench*, on the other hand, is usually used to describe something that smells bad. Your old shoes or last week's garbage, for example, might have a stench.

Why: Writers want to make sure that the reader feels a certain way when reading a group of words. As a result, good writers need to be aware of the emotional response connected to words in order to achieve the intended purpose for writing.

When: Good writers consider the connotations of every word. They are always thinking of hidden meanings and how the reader will respond to their writing.

How: Sometimes it may be necessary to consult a thesaurus or dictionary to determine if you are using the exact word you want. Consider the sample paragraphs provided below. One is written to give a positive impression of Mabel. The other is written to make the reader think she is not very attractive. Can you tell which is which?

SAMPLE A

Mabel's long, brown hair is straight. Her chocolate brown eyes exactly match the shade of her flowing hair. Her creamy skin is smooth. She has a short, button nose that compliments her facial features. Her cherry red lips reveal her pearly white teeth when she smiles.

SAMPLE B

Mabel's long, brown hair is stringy. Her muddy brown eyes exactly match the shade of her oily hair. Her dull, pale skin is smooth. She has a short, pug nose that goes with the rest of her chubby face. Her chapped lips reveal her chalky teeth when she smiles.

Standards and Benchmarks: 2A

Student Practice Sheet One

Consider the connotation of each pair of words. Write a plus sign (+) next to the word that has the more positive connotation. Write a minus sign (–) next to the word that has the more negative connotation.

	+/–		+/–
1. proud		stuck up	
2. lazy		unmotivated	
3. unusual		weird	
4. weak		wimpy	
5. stubborn		determined	

Write the word that has the more negative connotation.

6. look or stare? _____

7. adventurous or risky? _____

8. slow or cautious? _____

9. antique car or clunker? _____

10. fast food or junk food? _____

11. sweat or perspire? _____

12. con or convince? _____

Look at the words shown below. For each word provided, think of another word that has a similar meaning but a negative connotation.

13. hungry or_____   17. old or_____

14. curious or _____   18. tired or_____

15. loud or_____   19. bold or_____

16. wealthy or _____   20. alone or_____

- -
Note: Fold under before reproducing.

Answer Key

1. proud	+	stuck up	–
2. lazy	–	unmotivated	+
3. unusual	+	weird	–
4. weak	+	wimpy	–
5. stubborn	–	determined	+

6. stare   7. risky   8. slow   9. clunker   10. junk food   11. sweat   12. con

Standards and Benchmarks: 2A

Student Practice Sheet Two

Pretend you are a salesperson trying to sell the following items. Write a sales pitch, paying particular attention to the connotation of words.

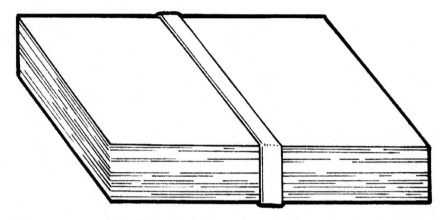

Here is an example: *a rubber band—This springy, elastic fastener, with its strength and durability, will control even your most unruly papers.*

1. a pencil sharpener _____

2. toothpaste _____

3. a pair of scissors _____

4. a lamp _____

5. shampoo _____

6. a pillow _____

7. a blanket _____

8. a pair of earrings _____

9. a coat hanger _____

10. a television _____

11. a pair of slippers _____

12. a pair of jeans _____

13. a towel _____

14. a bar of soap _____

15. a box of crayons _____

Showing, Not Telling
Teaching Guide

Goal: The students will provide elaboration to describe specific actions and appearances rather than making simple statements in descriptive writing.

Introducing the Skill

Preparation: Reproduce the Student Resource Sheet (page 38) for students and make a copy for yourself to use as a teaching reference.

Directions: Distribute the Student Resource Sheet to students. Tell students WHAT skill they will be learning. Explain WHY writers use this skill and WHY it will make your students' writing better. Show several examples of WHEN this skill is used. Teach students HOW to use this skill.

Practicing the Skill

Preparation: Reproduce the Student Practice Sheets (pages 39 and 40) for students.

Directions: Assign the practice sheets to students according to their needs and abilities. You may wish to have students work on these sheets in one or more of the following ways: as a whole-class activity, with a partner, in small groups, or independently. As an alternative, you may prefer to use one or both sheets as homework assignments. Provide feedback to students to ensure mastery of the skill.

Applying the Skill

Preparation: Write simple statements, such as those shown below, on slips of paper. You will need enough slips for each student in the class to have one. Place the slips in a container, such as a hat, bag, or small box.

- The woman was angry.
- The mother was proud of her son.
- The dog was hungry.
- The doctor performed the operation.

Directions: Engage students in a game of charades. Choose a student to select a slip of paper from the container. Instruct that student to read the sentence on the slip of paper to him/herself. The student should then "act out" the sentence for the class. Discuss how to use facial expressions, body movements, props, etc. The rest of the class should try to guess what the sentence on the slip of paper says based on the performance. Continue with the game until all students have had a chance to act out a sentence.

Student Resource Sheet

What: Good writers show the reader what is happening, rather than just telling what is going on.

Why: Showing the reader what is happening is much more descriptive and interesting than simply making a statement without any details or descriptions.

When: Good writers show their readers what is happening all the time.

How: Think about what the scene would look like if actors were portraying it. Think about how the characters would look, what their facial expressions would be, where they would be, how they would speak, etc. Show the reader what is happening by writing with action, feeling, and description. Below are some examples. Notice the difference between sentences that tell and those that show.

Telling: Julie is a bully.

Showing: Julie intentionally stuck out her leg as Timmy walked by. As Timmy tripped, Julie laughed in his face. "Gotcha again, Timmy-boy!" she jeered.

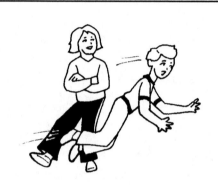

Telling: The house needed repair.

Showing: With shutters flapping in the wind, the house looked as if no one had lived there in years. The paint was peeling, the shrubs were overgrown, and several shingles were missing off the roof.

Telling: The man had a bad cold.

Showing: The man wheezed, coughed, and gasped for breath as he waited in the doctor's office.

Standards and Benchmarks: 2A, 2C, 3F, 3L

Student Practice Sheet One

Write a sentence describing what someone would **do** if he or she were feeling . . .

1. excited _____
2. sad _____
3. tired _____
4. hungry _____
5. angry _____
6. sick _____
7. bored _____
8. lonely _____
9. silly _____
10. lost _____

Write a sentence describing how someone would **look** if he or she were feeling . . .

11. excited _____
12. sad _____
13. tired _____
14. hungry _____
15. angry _____
16. sick _____
17. bored _____
18. lonely _____
19. silly _____
20. lost _____

Pick five of the words from above. On a separate sheet of paper, write a sentence that shows how the person acts and looks.

Here is an example: *excited—Sally jumped in the air and screamed with joy as she heard her name called as the sweepstakes winner.*

Showing, Not Telling

Standards and Benchmarks: 2A, 2C, 3F, 3L

Student Practice Sheet Two

Rewrite the following sentences, changing them from telling sentences to showing sentences.

1. The puppy is cute. _____
_____
_____

2. My teacher is so nice. _____
_____
_____

3. The house looked abandoned. _____
_____
_____

4. My little brother is helpful. _____
_____
_____

5. This is an exciting game. _____
_____
_____

6. The flowers were beautiful. _____
_____
_____

7. The man was scared. _____
_____
_____

8. School lunches are gross. _____
_____
_____

9. Sharon had a great costume. _____
_____
_____

10. The girl was exhausted. _____
_____
_____

Using a Thesaurus
Teaching Guide

Goal: The students will enhance their writing by using a thesaurus to locate precise and descriptive words.

Introducing the Skill

Preparation: Obtain a thesaurus for each student or pair of students in your class.

Directions: Ask students to brainstorm words that mean *nice*. They will probably only come up with a few, such as *friendly* and *kind*. Explain to students that, like a dictionary, a thesaurus is a valuable tool to writers. It helps writers find other words to use so that they can be precise and more descriptive when they write. Allow students time to flip through the thesauri to see how these books are set up. Depending on the level of your students, you may wish to structure this with a "guided tour" of the thesaurus. To do this, you simply point out how the thesaurus is set up and ask them to look at examples in their thesauri.

Practicing the Skill

Preparation: Reproduce the Student Practice Sheets (pages 42 and 43) for students.

Directions: Assign the practice sheets to students according to their needs and abilities. You may wish to have students work on these sheets in one or more of the following ways: as a whole-class activity, with a partner, in small groups, or independently. As an alternative, you may prefer to use one or both sheets as homework assignments. Provide feedback to students to ensure mastery of the skill.

Applying the Skill

Preparation: Using a thesaurus and a copy of the Teacher Resource Sheet (page 44), create a bank of words that are listed as alternatives for six target words such as *eat, make, help, drink, break,* and *fix*. The words you include in the word bank will depend on what is listed in the thesauri your class is using. Write the target words in the small boxes labeled *Word 1, Word 2, Word 3,* etc. Then list in the Word Bank box every synonym that is listed for these target words in the thesaurus. Make sure to write the synonyms in random order. Then reproduce the Word Bank you have created for students.

Directions: Distribute the Word Bank to students. Review the target words with the class. Then inform students that the words in the Word Bank box are synonyms for the target words. Challenge students to sort the synonyms by listing each under the appropriate target word. Students will automatically know some of the synonyms. For an unfamiliar word, direct students to look it up in the thesaurus so they are able to determine under which target word it should be listed.

Standards and Benchmarks: 2A

Student Practice Sheet One

Read the following dialogue between a mother and her son. Then read the dialogue below the box. You will notice that the second dialogue is the same, but the word *said* has been left out. Use a thesaurus to find a different synonym to replace the word *said* each time it was used. Write the new words in the blanks.

"Tommy, time for dinner," said Mom.

"Aww, Mom, I was just starting to have fun," said Tommy. "Nobody else has to eat dinner yet," he said.

"Your father has an important meeting tonight, so we need to eat early," said Mom. "Please come inside right now," she said.

"After we eat, can I go back outside?" asked Tommy.

"We'll have to see if it's still light out," said Mom. "I don't want you playing outside after dark," she said. "Maybe you could play inside with your sister, instead," Mom said.

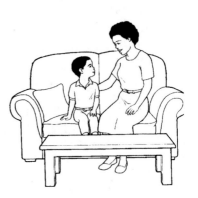

"No way! That's torture!" said Tommy.

"Tommy! That's not very nice," said Mom.

"Just kidding," Tommy said with a smile.

"Tommy, time for dinner," _____ Mom.

"Aww, Mom, I was just starting to have fun," _____ Tommy. "Nobody else has to eat dinner yet," he _____.

"Your father has an important meeting tonight, so we need to eat early," _____ Mom. "Please come inside right now," she _____.

"After we eat, can I go back outside?" asked Tommy.

"We'll have to see if it's still light out," _____ Mom. "I don't want you playing outside after dark," she _____. "Maybe you could play inside with your sister, instead," Mom _____.

"No way! That's torture!" _____ Tommy.

"Tommy! That's not very nice," _____ Mom.

"Just kidding," Tommy _____ with a smile.

Standards and Benchmarks: 2A

Student Practice Sheet Two

The list of "tired" words shown below have been used so often in writing that they have been worn out and are no longer effective. Look up each "tired" word in a thesaurus. Underneath each "tired" word, list synonyms that are much more interesting and descriptive. Save this worksheet after you finish it so you can easily refer to these synonyms. Using a variety of words will help make your writing more interesting.

bad	**good**

pretty	**ugly**

happy	**old**

boring	**fun**

Teacher Resource Sheet

Word Bank

Read the list of words in the Word Bank above. These are synonyms for the target words provided below. Using a thesaurus as a reference tool, sort the words in the Word Bank by listing each synonym under the appropriate target word. Not every target word has eight synonyms. As a result, some boxes under the target words will be blank.

Word 1:	

Word 2:	

Word 3:	

Word 4:	

Word 5:	

Word 6:	

Commas in a Series
Teaching Guide

Goal: The students will use commas to correctly punctuate items in a series.

Introducing the Skill

Preparation: Reproduce the Student Resource Sheet (page 46) for students and make a copy for yourself to use as a teaching reference.

Directions: Distribute the Student Resource Sheet to students. Tell students WHAT skill they will be learning. Explain WHY writers use this skill and WHY it will make your students' writing better. Show several examples of WHEN this skill is used. Teach students HOW to use this skill.

Practicing the Skill

Preparation: Reproduce the Student Practice Sheets (pages 47 and 48) for students.

Directions: Assign the practice sheets to students according to their needs and abilities. You may wish to have students work on these sheets in one or more of the following ways: as a whole-class activity, with a partner, in small groups, or independently. As an alternative, you may prefer to use one or both sheets as homework assignments. Provide feedback to students to ensure mastery of the skill.

Applying the Skill

Preparation: For this activity, you will need six sentence strips, five or six "comma clothespins," and a large resealable plastic bag for each group of three or four students. On the sentence strips, write sentences that include several items in a series. Do NOT include any commas. Using a permanent black marker, draw a comma on the "mouth" end of each clothespin. For each group of students, place six sentence strips and five or six "comma clothespins" in a large resealable plastic bag.

Directions: Divide the class into cooperative groups with three or four students in each. Provide each group of students with a bag of sentence strips and "comma clothespins." Instruct students to read aloud the sentences on the strips, one at a time. Tell them to insert commas in each sentence where they are needed by attaching the "comma clothespins" on the correct spot of the sentence strip.

I went to the store to buy cheese, eggs, and milk.

Student Resource Sheet

What: Good writers use commas to separate items in a series or list.

Why: Commas show the reader where to pause, and they help keep the reader from becoming confused by words that might otherwise get jumbled together.

When: Put commas in a sentence when you have a list of three or more items.

How: Put commas in between the items in your list. This tells the reader to pause after each item.

Here is an example. *I went to the store to buy cheese, eggs, and milk.*

This person bought three things at the store.

  1. cheese   2. eggs   3. milk

The commas separating the items help the reader understand the sentence and easily identify what was bought.

Here is another example. This one is a bit trickier. Sometimes two or more words will be considered to be one item.

In the following sentence, the writer is again listing three items: *For lunch you could have a peanut butter and jelly, ham and cheese, or tuna fish sandwich.*

In this case, the writer is offering three types of sandwiches.

  1. peanut butter and jelly   2. ham and cheese   3. tuna fish

The commas separating the items help the reader easily identify what the three choices are.

Here are some more examples for your reference.

- Last summer I visited Paris, London, Rome, and Venice.
- My room has clothes hanging in the closet, laying on the bed, and thrown on the floor!
- In math class, we learned how to add fractions, multiply two-digit numbers, and convert centimeters to meters.
- We could go shopping at the mall, see a movie at the theater, or rent a video to watch at home.
- I had macaroni and cheese, salad, and a glass of milk for dinner.

Standards and Benchmarks: 3D, 3L

Student Practice Sheet One

Insert commas in the following sentences where they are needed.

1. Whales dogs and elephants are all mammals.

2. My favorite sports are baseball soccer and karate.

3. My mom made turkey stuffing mashed potatoes and green beans for dinner.

4. France Spain and Italy are countries in Europe.

5. George Washington Abraham Lincoln and Theodore Roosevelt have all been Presidents of the United States of America.

6. Delaware Pennsylvania Massachusetts Connecticut and New York were all part of the original 13 colonies.

7. I invited John Mike and Hannah to my party.

8. I went to the movies with Larry Thompson Martin O'Malley Pauline Peterson and Chelsea Obermeier.

9. Do you want to go fishing to the movies or skateboarding this weekend?

10. When I get home from school, I eat a nutritious snack change my clothes finish my homework and go outside to play.

11. I like mushrooms pepperoni and sausage on my pizza.

12. Fluffy Rags and Buddy are the names of my three dogs.

Note: Fold under before reproducing.

Answer Key

1. Whales, dogs, and elephants are all mammals.
2. My favorite sports are baseball, soccer, and karate.
3. My mom made turkey, stuffing, mashed potatoes, and green beans for dinner.
4. France, Spain, and Italy are countries in Europe.
5. George Washington, Abraham Lincoln, and Theodore Roosevelt have all been Presidents of the United States of America.
6. Delaware, Pennsylvania, Massachusetts, Connecticut, and New York were all part of the original 13 colonies.
7. I invited John, Mike, and Hannah to my party.
8. I went to the movies with Larry Thompson, Martin O'Malley, Pauline Peterson, and Chelsea Obermeier.
9. Do you want to go fishing, to the movies, or skateboarding this weekend?
10. When I get home from school, I eat a nutritious snack, change my clothes, finish my homework, and go outside to play.
11. I like mushrooms, pepperoni, and sausage on my pizza.
12. Fluffy, Rags, and Buddy are the names of my three dogs.

Standards and Benchmarks: 3D, 3L

Student Practice Sheet Two

Complete the following sentences by writing a series of appropriate items in the blanks. Write at least three items in each blank. Be sure to insert commas where they are needed.

1. I like to _____ when I am on vacation.

2. My hobbies are _____.

3. _____ are my favorite foods.

4. My favorite school subjects are _____.

5. _____ are my least favorite school subjects.

6. My best friends are _____.

7. On my last birthday, I _____.

8. I like to _____ on the weekends.

9. I have _____ in my room.

10. I like _____ on my pizza.

11. My favorite colors are _____.

12. If I could have any three skills that I don't have now, _____

    _____would be what I would choose.

13. _____ are my role models.

14. The people in my family are _____.

15. When I grow up I want to be _____.

16. _____ are my favorite television shows.

17. _____ are my favorite songs.

18. I wish _____.

19. I am afraid of _____.

20. When I get home from school, I like to _____

    _____.

Prepositional Phrases
Teaching Guide

Goal: The students will elaborate and clarify descriptive writing using prepositional phrases.

Introducing the Skill

Preparation: Reproduce the Student Resource Sheet (pages 50 and 51) for students and make a copy for yourself to use as a teaching reference.

Directions: Distribute the Student Resource Sheet to students. Tell students WHAT skill they will be learning. Explain WHY writers use this skill and WHY it will make your students' writing better. Show several examples of WHEN this skill is used. Teach students HOW to use this skill.

Practicing the Skill

Preparation: Reproduce the Student Practice Sheets (pages 52 and 53) for students.

Directions: Assign the practice sheets to students according to their needs and abilities. You may wish to have students work on these sheets in one or more of the following ways: as a whole-class activity, with a partner, in small groups, or independently. As an alternative, you may prefer to use one or both sheets as homework assignments. Provide feedback to students to ensure mastery of the skill.

Applying the Skill

Preparation: None

Directions: Ask students to write directions to the kitchen in their homes, starting at their bedroom doors. Inform students that they can only use prepositional phrases in their directions. You may wish to do an example together, such as giving directions from the classroom door to the nearest water fountain.

Directions to the Kitchen
1. out the door
2. to the right
3. down the hall
4. around the corner
5. up the stairs
6. below the clock

Student Resource Sheet

What: Good writers use prepositional phrases in sentences to give more information. A preposition is a word that shows how one or more other words are related to the subject of the sentence. A prepositional phrase includes a preposition and other words to help clarify this relationship.

Why: Prepositional phrases help writers provide additional information and elaborate on a subject. Elaboration helps the reader better understand what the sentence is about and shows the relationship of the subject to other words in the sentence.

When: Prepositional phrases can be used at the beginning, in the middle, or at the end of a sentence. Prepositional phrases can be used any time the writer needs to provide more information about a subject.

How: Think about the relationship between the two words that are being described.

Here is an example.

> If a writer is describing the location to tell where a baseball bat hit the baseball, the writer could use the following prepositional phrase:
>
> *The bat hit the ball **on the stitching**, and the ball sailed into the outfield.*
>
> The prepositional phrase lets the reader know exactly where the bat hit the ball.

Here are some more examples:

The hat is **on his head**.

The hat is **under the table**.

The hat is **between the chairs**.

The hat is **above the door**.

The boy walked **through his neighbor's yard**.

The boy walked **underneath the ladder**.

The boy walked **toward the ball**.

The boy walked **down the stairs.**

Across from the school is a store.

In front of the movie theater is a store.

On top of the mountain is a store.

Behind the trees is a store.

Student Resource Sheet *(cont.)*

Here are some commonly used prepositions.

about	from
above	in
across	into
after	like
against	of
along	off
amid	on
among	onto
around	over
at	past
before	since
behind	through
below	throughout
beneath	to
beside	toward
besides	under
between	underneath
beyond	until
by	unto
concerning	up
down	upon
during	with
except	within
for	without

Standards and Benchmarks: 2A, 2C, 3D, 3F, 3G

Student Practice Sheet One

Look at the following pictures. Write a sentence that describes the relationship of the subjects in the picture. Be sure to include a prepositional phrase.

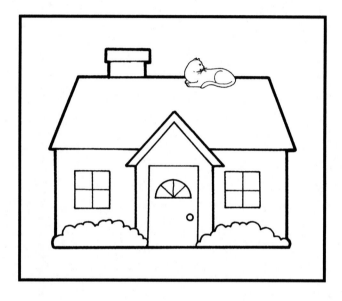

_____

_____

_____

_____

_____

_____

Standards and Benchmarks: 2A, 2C, 3D, 3F, 3G

Student Practice Sheet Two

Write a sentence that describes the relationship between each pair of items listed below. Be sure to include a prepositional phrase in each sentence.

1. a bell and a cow _____

2. a barn and a farmer _____

3. an airplane and a runway _____

4. a foot and a shoe _____

5. a pepperoni and a slice of pizza _____

6. a scarf and a snowman _____

7. a flag and a building _____

8. a dentist's drill and a tooth _____

9. a rattle and a baby _____

10. a dog and a bone _____

Now write a sentence using each of the following prepositions.

11. underneath _____

12. between _____

13. against _____

14. within _____

15. throughout _____

16. past _____

17. upon _____

18. after _____

Appositives

Teaching Guide

Goal: The students will use appositives to provide elaboration and clarification in descriptive writing.

Introducing the Skill

Preparation: Reproduce the Student Resource Sheet (page 55) for students and make a copy for yourself to use as a teaching reference.

Directions: Distribute the Student Resource Sheet to students. Tell students WHAT skill they will be learning. Explain WHY writers use this skill and WHY it will make your students' writing better. Show several examples of WHEN this skill is used. Teach students HOW to use this skill.

Practicing the Skill

Preparation: Reproduce the Student Practice Sheets (pages 56 and 57) for students.

Directions: Assign the practice sheets to students according to their needs and abilities. You may wish to have students work on these sheets in one or more of the following ways: as a whole-class activity, with a partner, in small groups, or independently. As an alternative, you may prefer to use one or both sheets as homework assignments. Provide feedback to students to ensure mastery of the skill.

Applying the Skill

Preparation: None

Directions: Ask students to list the people they want to invite to their next party by listing the person's first name and their relation to the student. Students should write a sentence about each person, including their relation. They should separate the name from the relation with commas, creating an appositive.

Write the following examples on the chalkboard to show students how appositives are formed:

- Tyler, my little brother, just started school.

- Sam, my best friend, is coming over to my house.

- Anna, my grandmother, lives in Georgia.

- Ms. Granger, my fifth-grade teacher, is retiring.

Student Resource Sheet

What: Good writers use appositives in sentences to give more information about a subject.

Why: Appositives help the writer provide additional information and elaborate on a subject. Elaboration helps the reader better understand who the subject is.

When: Appositives can be used at the beginning, in the middle, or at the end of a sentence. Appositives can be used any time the writer needs to provide more information about a subject.

How: An appositive is separated from the rest of the sentence by commas. Below are some sample sentences with appositives. The appositive is boldfaced. Remember, the appositive appears between a comma and the end punctuation or between two commas and explains more about the subject.

I had to feed my little sister, *a two-year-old toddler.*

my little sister = a two-year-old toddler

Rocko, *the prize fighter*, is waiting in the boxing ring.

Rocko = the prize fighter

She is the youngest child, *one of four brothers and sisters*.

She = one of four brothers and sisters

It went away slowly, *the sick feeling that overcame me*.

It = the sick feeling that overcame me

On my way to the kitchen, I found my pet snake, *a garden variety that is no bigger than my hand*.

my pet snake = a garden variety that is no bigger than my hand

---

Standards and Benchmarks: 3D, 3K, 3L

Student Practice Sheet One

Read the following sentences. Decide if they contain appositives. Write *Yes* or *No* in the blank before each sentence to tell whether or not it has an appositive.

Yes/No

_____ 1. I dreamed about my friend, Sam.

_____ 2. My fourth-grade teacher, Mrs. Smith, just had a baby.

_____ 3. I ordered a hamburger, and I added ketchup and mustard to it.

_____ 4. Sharks, dolphins, and colorful fish swim in the ocean.

_____ 5. The bride carried fresh flowers, a beautiful bouquet of roses and lilies.

_____ 6. We watched Kelly, a graceful ballerina, glide across the dance floor.

_____ 7. I play baseball, football, and soccer in my spare time.

_____ 8. Mr. Johnson, an ex-major league baseball player, is coaching my team.

_____ 9. At my party, we had pizza, cake, and punch.

_____ 10. I buttoned my coat, got my umbrella, and stepped out into the rain.

Now rewrite each sentence above that does not have an appositive. Be sure to change the sentence so that it includes an appositive this time.

_____

_____

_____

_____

_____

_____

_____

- -

Note: Fold under before reproducing.

Answer Key

Yes: 1, 2, 5, 6, 8

No: 3, 4, 7, 9, 10

Standards and Benchmarks: 3D, 3K, 3L

Student Practice Sheet Two

Combine each pair of sentences to create one sentence that contains an appositive.

1. I buttoned my raincoat. My raincoat is a bright yellow slicker.

   _____

2. I opened my present. My present was a brand new bicycle.

   _____

3. The tree was twenty feet tall. The tree was an evergreen.

   _____

4. Dave called me on the telephone. Dave is my best friend.

   _____

5. The pitcher threw a shutout. The pitcher was an eighteen-year-old rookie.

   _____

Expand the following sentences to include appositives.

Here is an example.

> The boy looked at them, _____.
>
> The boy looked at them, those big, ugly insects.
>
> *them = those big, ugly insects*

6. Paula, _____, got straight A's on her report card.

   (Think of something that Paula equals.)

7. Steve Howard, _____, scored the winning touchdown for the football team.

   (Think of something that Steve Howard equals.)

8. As they danced, in came Sherlock, _____.

   (Think of something that Sherlock equals.)

9. My cousin, _____, is a champion swimmer.

   (Think of something that my cousin equals.)

10. She put on her coat, _____.

    (Think of something that her coat equals.)

Sentence Structures: Using Colons
Teaching Guide

Goal: The students will use sophisticated sentence structures to expand their descriptions and make their writing more interesting.

Introducing the Skill

Preparation: Reproduce the Student Resource Sheet (pages 60 and 61) for students and make a copy for yourself to use as a teaching reference.

Directions: Distribute the Student Resource Sheet to students. Tell students WHAT skill they will be learning. Explain WHY writers use this skill and WHY it will make your students' writing better. Show several examples of WHEN this skill is used. Teach students HOW to use this skill.

Practicing the Skill

Preparation: Reproduce the Student Practice Sheets (pages 62 and 63) for students.

Directions: Assign the practice sheets to students according to their needs and abilities. You may wish to have students work on these sheets in one or more of the following ways: as a whole-class activity, with a partner, in small groups, or independently. As an alternative, you may prefer to use one or both sheets as homework assignments. Provide feedback to students to ensure mastery of the skill.

Applying the Skill

Preparation: Write colon sentences on sentence strips. Laminate the strips for durability. Cut the strips apart just after each colon. Place several cut sentences into a manila envelope. Make enough envelopes so each group of students will have one.

Directions: Divide the class into groups with three or four students in each. Provide one manila envelope to each group of students. Tell students that they have sentence puzzles inside the envelopes. Explain that their task is to piece together the sentence strips to form colon sentences. Remind students to read all of the strips before trying to put together the two parts that make each sentence. Point out that each complete sentence students create must make sense.

Here is an example.

We looked everywhere for my keys: / the car, the door, the kitchen counter, the floor.

(Cut here.)

Sentence Structures: Using Semicolons

Teaching Guide

Goal: The students will use sophisticated sentence structures to expand their descriptions and make their writing more interesting.

Introducing the Skill

Preparation: Reproduce the Student Resource Sheet (pages 60 and 61) for students and make a copy for yourself to use as a teaching reference.

Directions: Distribute the Student Resource Sheet to students. Tell students WHAT skill they will be learning. Explain WHY writers use this skill and WHY it will make your students' writing better. Show several examples of WHEN this skill is used. Teach students HOW to use this skill.

Practicing the Skill

Preparation: Reproduce the Student Practice Sheets (pages 64 and 65) for students.

Directions: Assign the practice sheets to students according to their needs and abilities. You may wish to have students work on these sheets in one or more of the following ways: as a whole-class activity, with a partner, in small groups, or independently. As an alternative, you may prefer to use one or both sheets as homework assignments. Provide feedback to students to ensure mastery of the skill.

Applying the Skill

Preparation: Write semicolon sentences on sentence strips. Laminate the strips for durability. Cut the strips apart just after each semicolon. Place several cut sentences into a manila envelope. Make enough envelopes so each group of students will have one.

Directions: Divide the class into groups with three or four students in each. Provide one manila envelope to each group of students. Tell students that they have sentence puzzles inside the envelopes. Explain that their task is to piece together the sentence strips to form semicolon sentences. Remind students to read all of the strips before trying to put together the two parts that make each sentence. Point out that each complete sentence students create must make sense.

Here is an example.

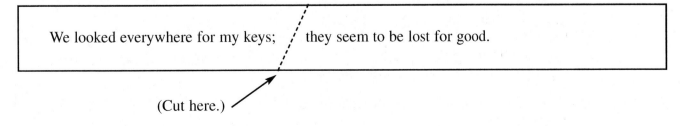

We looked everywhere for my keys; / they seem to be lost for good.

(Cut here.)

Student Resource Sheet

What: Good writers use sophisticated sentence structures in their writing. Colon sentences and semicolon sentences are sophisticated sentence structures.

Why: Good writers use sophisticated sentence structures in order to make their writing more interesting and informative to the reader.

When: Colon and semicolon sentences are used at different times. A colon sentence adds more information to an already complete sentence. Use a colon after a complete sentence when you want to list more information about the sentence. A semicolon sentence joins two complete sentences. Use a semicolon sentence when you have two sentences that are related and would make sense together.

How: For a colon sentence, first write a complete sentence. Instead of a period, put a colon (:) at the end of that sentence. After the colon, list more information about the sentence.

Here are some examples.

- *The mall has all kinds of shops: clothing stores, jewelry stores, shoe stores, and places to eat.*

  In this sentence, the first part "The mall has all kinds of shops," is a complete sentence by itself. However, the writer wanted to give more information, so a colon was used instead of a period. Then the writer listed some types of shops that are in the mall—"clothing stores, jewelry stores, shoe stores, and places to eat." The words after the colon give the reader more information.

- *The bouquet included three kinds of flowers: roses, carnations, and daisies.*

  The first part of this colon sentence is a complete sentence. The part after the colon gives more information about the sentence. It tells what kind of flowers were in the bouquet.

- *The streets were filled with people wearing costumes: clowns, famous people, and animals.*

  The part before the colon is a complete sentence. The second part tells what kind of costumes the people were wearing.

- *This is the perfect beach day: the sun is shining, the waves are small, and the sand is not too hot.*

  The part before the colon is a complete sentence. The second part tells what makes the day at the beach perfect.

- *Debbie dropped her purse and spilled its contents: lipstick, a comb, her wallet, some tissues, and a stick of gum.*

  The part before the colon is a complete sentence. The second part tells the contents of Debbie's purse.

Student Resource Sheet *(cont.)*

For a semicolon sentence, two related sentences are combined to make one longer sentence. Instead of a period between the two sentences, there is a semicolon (;).

Here are some examples of semicolon sentences.

- *Football is a dangerous sport; it is very easy for players to get hurt.*

  Notice that the first part, "Football is a dangerous sport," is a complete sentence. The author could have put a period at the end. The second part, "it is very easy for players to get hurt," is also a complete sentence. Because the two sentences are talking about the dangers of football, the writer combined the two sentences into one, using a semicolon.

- *Niagara Falls is the honeymoon capital of the world; many newlyweds visit it each year.*

  Both parts of this semicolon sentence are talking about Niagara Falls being a popular vacation location for newlyweds.

- *That night, Rose could not sleep; she was worried about her math test the next day.*

  Both parts of this semicolon sentence are talking about Rose not being able to sleep because she was worried.

- *The baseball field is lined and the hot dogs are cooked; opening day has finally arrived!*

  Both parts of this semicolon sentence are talking about opening day in baseball.

If two sentences are not related, do not join them with a semicolon. For example, the following sentences would not be good semicolon sentences because the two sentences are not related.

- *Snakes have no eyelids. They eat mice.*

  The first sentence is talking about snake eyelids. The second sentence is talking about what snakes eat. These sentences do not go together.

- *A new painting hung on my wall. I spent all of my money on groceries.*

  The first sentence is talking about a new painting. The second sentence is talking about spending money on groceries. These sentences do not go together.

Standards and Benchmarks: 2C, 3L

Student Practice Sheet One

Expand the following sentences by writing a list of items after the colon.

Here is an example. *My bedspread has many colors: blue, black, tan, yellow, and gray.*

1. I have five subjects in school: _____.

   (Tell what the subjects are.)

2. Six friends attended my last birthday party: _____.

   (Tell who the friends were.)

3. Mr. Kennedy has lived in many states: _____.

   (Tell what states he has lived in.)

4. My sister plays sports in college: _____.

   (Tell what sports she plays.)

5. Martin bought the ingredients for chocolate chip cookies at the grocery store:

   _____.

   (Tell what the ingredients were.)

6. The platter included different kinds of sandwich meat: _____.

   (Tell what kinds of meat were on the platter.)

7. There are different kinds of books: _____.

   (List some kinds of books.)

8. I woke up and got dressed: _____.

   (Tell what you did to get dressed.)

9. I have attended three different schools: _____.

   (Name three different schools.)

10. Leticia has four pets: _____.

    (Tell what her four pets are.)

Standards and Benchmarks: 2C, 3L

Student Practice Sheet Two

First read the list of items that appears after each colon below. Then write a beginning sentence before each colon.

Here are some examples of how this sentence could begin.

I'm allergic to many foods: peanuts, milk, beef, and eggs.

OR

I went to the grocery store for a few items: peanuts, milk, beef, and eggs.

OR

My cousin refuses to eat some foods: peanuts, milk, beef, and eggs.

1. _____ : vanilla, chocolate, and strawberry.

2. _____ : ballet lesson, tutoring, and soccer practice.

3. _____ : pink, purple, green, and blue.

4. _____ : California, Florida, and Hawaii.

5. _____ : Sharon, Luis, Juan, Lorinda, and Zach.

6. _____ : flutes, violins, clarinets, and trumpets.

7. _____ : Superman, Batman, and Wonder Woman.

8. _____ : bats, gloves, balls, and bases.

9. _____ : mittens, a scarf, a hat, snow boots, and a heavy coat.

10. _____ : rings, necklaces, bracelets, and earrings.

Standards and Benchmarks: 2C, 3L

Student Practice Sheet One

Decide which of the following pairs of sentences are related. Write *Yes* in the blank if the pairs are related and would make a good semicolon sentence. Write *No* in the blank if the pairs are not related and would not make a good semicolon sentence.

Yes/No

_____ 1. I ate a chicken sandwich for lunch. I should play baseball more.

_____ 2. My doctor said I have asthma. Sometimes I will need to use an inhaler to help me breathe.

_____ 3. I hate cleaning my house. I'm thinking about hiring a cleaning lady.

_____ 4. My family went on a vacation last summer. I like to exercise.

_____ 5. The storm clouds appeared without warning. It started to pour down rain.

_____ 6. After the race, I was exhausted. I went right to bed.

_____ 7. I studied French for four years. Spain is my favorite vacation spot.

_____ 8. Many people are afraid of spiders. Cobwebs are sticky.

_____ 9. Horses are gentle animals. Saddles are made of leather.

_____ 10. Walt Disney created Mickey Mouse. Walt Disney created Minnie Mouse, too.

Write five semicolon sentences of your own.

11. _____

12. _____

13. _____

14. _____

15. _____

- -

Note: Fold under before reproducing.

Answer Key

1. No   2. Yes   3. Yes   4. No   5. Yes   6. Yes   7. No   8. No   9. No   10. Yes

Standards and Benchmarks: 2C, 3L

Student Practice Sheet Two

Finish the following semicolon sentences. Remember, a semicolon sentence is made of two complete sentences. Write a complete sentence that is related to the first sentence after the semicolon. Do not capitalize the first word of the second sentence.

Here is an example. *Crystal icicles clung to the tree branches; snow blanketed the ground.*

1. The clarinet is a wind instrument; _____

   _____.

2. My dog is playful; _____

   _____.

3. Many families visit Disneyworld when they are on vacation; _____

   _____.

4. I put cat food and water in the bowls for my cat; _____

   _____.

5. The hurricane was powerful; _____

   _____.

6. Mice like cheese; _____

   _____.

7. The pirate jumped aboard the ship; _____

   _____.

8. Mariah knits beautiful sweaters; _____

   _____.

9. We saw monkeys and elephants at the circus; _____

   _____.

10. The rainforest has a humid climate; _____

    _____.

Transitions
Teaching Guide

Goal: The students will use transitions to link ideas and clarify descriptive writing.

Introducing the Skill

Preparation: Reproduce the Student Resource Sheet (page 67) for students and make a copy for yourself to use as a teaching reference.

Directions: Distribute the Student Resource Sheet to students. Tell students WHAT skill they will be learning. Explain WHY writers use this skill and WHY it will make your students' writing better. Show several examples of WHEN this skill is used. Teach students HOW to use this skill.

Practicing the Skill

Preparation: Reproduce the Student Practice Sheets (pages 68 and 69) for students.

Directions: Assign the practice sheets to students according to their needs and abilities. You may wish to have students work on these sheets in one or more of the following ways: as a whole-class activity, with a partner, in small groups, or independently. As an alternative, you may prefer to use one or both sheets as homework assignments. Provide feedback to students to ensure mastery of the skill.

Applying the Skill

Preparation: Obtain highlighters or colored pencils for students. Reproduce some pages from a piece of literature your students have read or are currently reading. **Note:** Make sure the selection you choose has some transition words in it.

Directions: Distribute to students the sample pages from the literature selection you have chosen. Instruct students to scan the text, looking for transition words. Have them highlight or underline any transition words they find. Invite students to share their findings with the class.

Student Resource Sheet

What: Good writers use transitions when writing. Transitions are words and phrases that connect ideas.

Why: Transitions help the sentences flow together. Transitions make it easier for the reader to see connections between ideas.

When: Transitions can occur between or within sentences.

How: Transitions can be placed at the beginning, middle, or end of a sentence. Transition words are often punctuated with a comma.

Here are some examples of transition words.

additionally	in addition
afterwards	in place of
also	instead of
although	lastly
as a result	later
before	next
consequently	rather than
first	then
for example	therefore
furthermore	too
however	finally

Here are some examples of transitions used in sentences.

- I went to the store to get some bread. I got a jar of peanut butter, **also**.

- We had a baseball parade Saturday morning. **Afterwards**, we played our first game of the season.

- I was sick on Saturday afternoon. **Therefore**, I couldn't go to the movies with my friends.

Standards and Benchmarks: 2C, 3H, 3L

Student Practice Sheet One

Circle the transitions in the following sentences.

1. I like to read. I like to do crafts, also.

2. Instead of cooking dinner, we went out to eat.

3. I take piano lessons in addition to clarinet lessons.

4. First I went to the mall with my mother. Then I went to the movies with my friends.

5. My older sister talks on the phone constantly. Therefore, our line is always busy.

6. My teacher is very nice. For example, she sends us cards in the mail on our birthdays.

7. Rather than stay up to watch the movie on television, I went to bed and read a little of my book.

8. My family lives in Maryland. Before that, we lived in New York.

9. I'm not a very good cook. However, I can make a great grilled cheese sandwich.

10. At the amusement park, we rode the roller coaster, the carousel, the water slide, and finally, the monorail.

Complete the following sentences, adding more information before or after the transition.

11. I love roses. _____, also.

12. My brother plays basketball. However, _____.

13. First _____. Then _____.

14. Although _____, I ate it anyway.

15. Before _____, we ate dinner.

16. We had a social studies test in addition to _____.

17. Rather than _____, I got up and left.

18. We built a snowman in the back yard. Afterwards, _____.

19. I know how to do magic tricks. For example, _____.

20. Instead of _____, I had a peanut butter and jelly sandwich.

- -

Note: Fold under before reproducing.

Answer Key

The following words should be circled.

1. also	4. first, then	7. rather than	9. however
2. instead	5. therefore	8. before that	10. finally
3. in addition	6. for example		

Standards and Benchmarks: 2C, 3H, 3L

Student Practice Sheet Two

Complete the following paragraphs, writing transitions in the blanks as appropriate. You may wish to use the Transition Word Bank for ideas.

Yesterday was such a bad day. _____ my alarm clock didn't go off. _____, because I was late, I didn't have time to take a shower. _____ my hair wouldn't comb the way I wanted it to. I couldn't find the pants I wanted to wear, so I had to wear the same ones as yesterday. That didn't matter, _____, since they were still pretty clean. _____, at breakfast, there was no milk for my cereal. I ended up eating it dry. _____ there was no orange juice. "Great," I thought, "I'm going to be ugly and hungry today."

I left the house to go catch the school bus. _____, I didn't realize I left my lunch on the kitchen counter until I was halfway to the bus stop. _____ the bus was late and I ended up standing around waiting for it. If only I could have gone back home to get my lunch. I probably would have had time after all.

When I got to school, my friend reminded me about the science test we were having. I had forgotten all about it. What else could go wrong? _____, I couldn't wait for this day to be over!

Transition Word Bank

additionally	finally	instead of
afterwards	first	lastly
also	for example	later
although	furthermore	next
as a result	however	then
before	in addition to	therefore
consequently	in place of	too

Standards and Benchmarks: 2A, 2C, 3D, 3F

Similes
Teaching Guide

Goal: The students will use similes to make comparisons that provide clarification and elaboration in descriptive writing.

Introducing the Skill

Preparation: Reproduce the Student Resource Sheet (page 71) for students and make a copy for yourself to use as a teaching reference.

Directions: Distribute the Student Resource Sheet to students. Tell students WHAT skill they will be learning. Explain WHY writers use this skill and WHY it will make your students' writing better. Show several examples of WHEN this skill is used. Teach students HOW to use this skill.

Practicing the Skill

Preparation: Reproduce the Student Practice Sheets (pages 72 and 73) for students.

Directions: Assign the practice sheets to students according to their needs and abilities. You may wish to have students work on these sheets in one or more of the following ways: as a whole-class activity, with a partner, in small groups, or independently. As an alternative, you may prefer to use one or both sheets as homework assignments. Provide feedback to students to ensure mastery of the skill.

Applying the Skill

Preparation: None

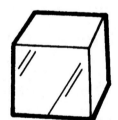

Directions: Write the following example on the chalkboard:

> Riddle: What is cold, cube-shaped, and as smooth as glass?

> Answer: An ice cube is cold, cube-shaped, and as smooth as glass.

Point out that the smoothness of an ice cube is compared to that of glass. Tell students that this type of comparison is called a simile. Explain that similes compare two things using the words *like* or *as*.

Assign partners or allow students to choose their own. Instruct the pairs of students to take turns creating and solving riddles. Explain that these riddles should contain similes like the example you have written on the chalkboard.

When pairs of students have created several riddles, lead the class in a riddle-telling session. Have the pairs of students ask their riddles and invite the rest of the class to solve them. You may wish to record a list of the similes in the riddles for future student reference.

Student Resource Sheet

What: Good writers use similes to make comparisons between subjects and other things.

Why: Good writers use similes to paint a more vivid mental picture for the reader. A simile helps the reader better understand the subject by comparing it to something else with which the reader might be familiar.

When: Writers can use similes at almost any point in their writing. Similes work best when the writer wants to use a comparison to help describe something more clearly.

How: Use similes at the beginning, middle, or end of a sentence. Similes compare two things using the words *like* or *as*. Below are some examples. Notice how the second sentence (the one with the simile) makes the description better by providing more information through a comparison.

She is quiet.
She is as quiet **as a mouse**.

After exercising, John's face was red.
After exercising, John's face was as red **as a tomato**.

She slept after the long day at the amusement park.
She slept **like a baby** after the long day at the amusement park.

The books toppled off the shelf.
The books toppled off the shelf **like a row of dominoes**.

He has spiky, brown hair.
His spiky, brown hair is **like porcupine quills**.

The children moved from place to place excitedly in their preschool classroom.
The children were **like bees,** buzzing from place to place in their preschool classroom.

She walked down the stairs gracefully in the fashion show.
She was as graceful **as a ballerina**, floating down the stairs in the fashion show.

The stars glistened in the dark night.
The stars were **like diamonds**, glistening in the dark night.

Standards and Benchmarks: 2A, 2C, 3D, 3F

Student Practice Sheet One

A simile is used to compare two things. Similes use the words *like* or *as* to show how the items are alike.

Here are some examples of similes.

- Her teeth are as white as snow.

  Her teeth are white, and snow is white.

- The snake was like a black garden hose.

  The snake was thin and black and lying in the grass.
  The garden hose was also thin and black and lying in the grass.

Explain the comparisons in the following similes:

1. The baby's red cheeks were like roses.

   The baby's cheeks are _____ and roses are _____.

2. The full moon is like a cookie.

   The full moon is _____ and a cookie is _____.

3. The cat purred like a motor boat.

   The cat _____ and a motor boat _____.

4. The coffee was as black as ink.

   Coffee is _____ and ink is _____.

5. The construction worker is as strong as an ox.

   The construction worker is _____ and an ox is _____.

6. The girl's hands are as cold as ice.

   The girl's hands are _____ and ice is _____.

   Now you try it. Write some similes of your own.

7. The boat is _____.

8. The cave is _____.

9. The child's hair is _____.

10. The horse is _____.

Read your similes to a friend. See if your friend can explain your comparisons.

Standards and Benchmarks: 2A, 2C, 3D, 3F

Student Practice Sheet Two

Expand the following similes by adding an action or a little more description.

Here is an example: *She was as happy as a lark,* **singing on a warm summer's day**.

1. The lava was like a geyser, _____

_____.

2. The woman's teeth were as white as pearls, _____

_____.

3. My mind was like a sponge, _____

_____.

4. My feet felt like ice cubes, _____

_____.

5. The little girl was as sweet as pie, _____

_____.

6. The boy's hair looked like wet spaghetti, _____

_____.

7. The nurse's eyes were like diamonds, _____

_____.

8. The rainbow looked like a box of crayons, _____

_____.

9. The hurricane was like a warrior, _____

_____.

10. The singer's voice was as deep as a bullfrog's, _____

_____.

Metaphors
Teaching Guide

Goal: The students will use metaphors to make comparisons that provide clarification and elaboration in descriptive writing.

Introducing the Skill

Preparation: Reproduce the Student Resource Sheet (page 75) for students and make a copy for yourself to use as a teaching reference.

Directions: Distribute the Student Resource Sheet to students. Tell students WHAT skill they will be learning. Explain WHY writers use this skill and WHY it will make your students' writing better. Show several examples of WHEN this skill is used. Teach students HOW to use this skill.

Practicing the Skill

Preparation: Reproduce the Student Practice Sheets (pages 76 and 77) for students.

Directions: Assign the practice sheets to students according to their needs and abilities. You may wish to have students work on these sheets in one or more of the following ways: as a whole-class activity, with a partner, in small groups, or independently. As an alternative, you may prefer to use one or both sheets as homework assignments. Provide feedback to students to ensure mastery of the skill.

Applying the Skill

Preparation: Reproduce the Student Worksheet (page 78) for students. Collect several common objects such as a toothbrush, a stapler, a pair of scissors, a marker, a sock, a staple remover, an eraser, a paper clip, a bar of soap, etc.

Directions: Place objects on a table or some other surface that can be easily viewed by students. Pick up an object and ask students to tell you what it is. Then ask students to think of the object differently, more creatively. Ask them to think of what the object could be. Provided the following examples: *A staple remover could be the jaws of a monster, ripping into its prey. A toothbrush could be a mop that cleans the white tile floor in a mouth.* Then distribute the Student Worksheet for students to record their thoughts as you display the objects. You may wish to have students work in pairs or small groups since this activity requires some extended, creative thinking.

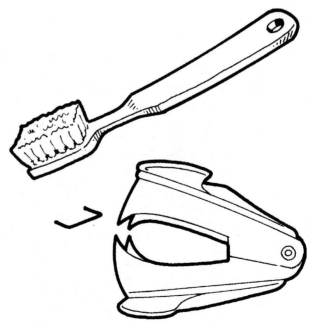

Student Resource Sheet

What: Good writers use metaphors to make comparisons between subjects and other things.

Why: Good writers use metaphors to paint a more vivid mental picture for the reader. A metaphor helps the reader better understand the subject by comparing it to something else with which the reader might be familiar.

When: Writers can use metaphors at almost any point in their writing. Metaphors work best when the writer wants to use a comparison to help describe something more clearly.

How: Use metaphors at the beginning, middle, or end of a sentence. Unlike similes, metaphors do NOT use the words *like* or *as* to compare things. Below are some examples. Notice how the second sentence (the one with the metaphor) makes the description more vivid through a comparison.

She was quiet.
She **was a quiet mouse**, slinking through the abandoned house.

After exercising, the student's face was red.
After exercising, the student's face **was a tomato**.

The books toppled off the shelf.
The books **were a row of dominoes**, toppling off the shelf.

The boy has spiky, brown hair.
The boy **has spiky brown porcupine quills** on top of his head.

The children moved excitedly from place to place in their preschool classroom.
The children **were bees**, buzzing from place to place in their preschool classroom.

She walked gracefully down the stairs in the fashion show.
She **was a graceful ballerina**, floating down the stairs in the fashion show.

The stars glistened in the dark night.
The stars **were diamonds**, glistening in the dark night.

Remember that metaphors are figurative language. They are not intended to make the reader think, for example, that the student's face really was a tomato or the boy's hair really is made of porcupine quills. Metaphors add description to help the reader visualize the subject.

Standards and Benchmarks: 2A, 2C, 3D, 3F

Student Practice Sheet One

The examples below use metaphors to describe friendship. The writer compares friendship to something else, and then explains the connection. This type of comparison is called a metaphor. The writer compares two things, without using the words *like* or *as*.

Friendship is **a special treasure**. It should be carefully guarded.
Friendship is **a mountain**. It makes you feel strong inside.
Friendship is **a roller coaster ride**. It has its ups and downs.

Explain the connection in each the following metaphors.

1. Friendship is the wind. _____

_____

2. Friendship is a rainbow. _____

_____

3. Friendship is a sailboat. _____

_____

Now write some metaphors of your own. Explain the connections.

4. Friendship is _____

_____

5. Time is _____

_____

6. Families are _____

_____

7. Anger is _____

_____

8. Happiness is _____

_____

Standards and Benchmarks: 2A, 2C, 3D, 3F

Student Practice Sheet Two

Create some mixed metaphors by choosing a noun from Column One and a noun from Column Two and writing them as a metaphor. Extend the metaphors you create by explaining the connection between the two nouns.

Here is an example. **Summertime** *is a* **race** *to see who can have the most fun.*

Column One	Column Two
love	jail
money	a dark cloud
summertime	freedom
school	a vacation
friends	a best friend
pizza	trophies
anger	music
dreams	an ocean
wrinkles	a race
jealousy	art
television	diamonds

1. _____

2. _____

3. _____

4. _____

5. _____

6. _____

7. _____

Student Worksheet

Examine the objects that your teacher shows you. In the left-hand column, write a description of what the object really is. In the right-hand column, write a metaphor that could be used to describe the object.

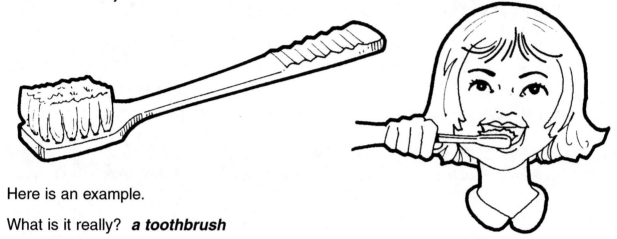

Here is an example.

What is it really? *a toothbrush*

What could it be metaphorically? *a mop to clean the shiny tile floor of my mouth*

What is it really?	What could it be metaphorically?
1.	1.
2.	2.
3.	3.
4.	4.
5.	5.
6.	6.
7.	7.
8.	8.
9.	9.
10.	10.

78

Onomatopoeia
Teaching Guide

Goal: The students will use onomatopoeia to enhance their descriptive writing.

Introducing the Skill

Preparation: Reproduce the Student Resource Sheet (page 80) for students and make a copy for yourself to use as a teaching reference.

Directions: Distribute the Student Resource Sheet to students. Tell students WHAT skill they will be learning. Explain WHY writers use this skill and WHY it will make your students' writing better. Show several examples of WHEN this skill is used. Teach students HOW to use this skill.

Practicing the Skill

Preparation: Reproduce the Student Practice Sheets (pages 81 and 82) for students.

Directions: Assign the practice sheets to students according to their needs and abilities. You may wish to have students work on these sheets in one or more of the following ways: as a whole-class activity, with a partner, in small groups, or independently. As an alternative, you may prefer to use one or both sheets as homework assignments. Provide feedback to students to ensure mastery of the skill.

Applying the Skill

Preparation: Reproduce the Group Storytelling Worksheet (pages 83 and 84) for each student in the class.

Directions: Read aloud the story on the Group Storytelling Worksheet to students, omitting the specified sound effects. Then distribute the copies of the worksheets to students and reread the story together. This time invite students to provide the sound effects called for in the story. Ask students which version was more interesting to listen to and seemed more "alive." Lead students to conclude that the version with onomatopoeia was much more interesting and caught their attention.

Student Resource Sheet

What: Good writers use onomatopoeia to add realistic sounds to their writing. Onomatopoeia uses words that sound like the objects or actions they are describing.

Why: Good writers use onomatopoeia to catch the reader's attention and make their writing seem more "alive."

When: Onomatopoeia can be used anytime you are writing about something that makes a certain noise and you want to include that sound in your writing.

How: Onomatopoeia is easy to use. You can just think of a word that sounds like what you are trying to describe and include it in your writing. It could be a real word like *buzz* or a made-up word like *umph*.

Below is a list of onomatopoeic words. You may wish to add others that you know.

bang	grate	slurp
beep	grind	smack
blink	gurgle	snap
boom	hiss	snip
bow wow	honk	splash
buzz	hum	squeak
chirp	meow	squeal
chug	moan	squish
clang	moo	swish
clap	muffle	tap
clatter	munch	thump
click	murmur	tick-tock
cluck	muzzle	warble
cough	ping	whack
crack	plop	whisk
crackle	quack	whisper
crash	rattle	whistle
creak	ring	yawn
crunch	rip	zoom
cuckoo	roar	_____
ding dong	rustle	_____
drip	shuffle	_____
fizz	sizzle	_____
flip flop	slam	_____
glug	slap	_____

Standards and Benchmarks: 2A

Student Practice Sheet One

What sound does each of the following animals make?

1. a cat _____

2. a duck _____

3. a dog _____

4. a sheep _____

5. a horse _____

6. a snake _____

What sound does each of the following objects make?

7. a train _____

8. the ocean _____

9. a balloon _____

10. a door _____

11. the wind _____

12. thunder _____

What sounds would you hear if you were . . .

13. watching a football game _____

14. bowling at a bowling alley _____

15. toasting a piece of bread _____

16. blowing a bubble with bubble gum _____

17. emptying a dishwasher _____

18. listening to a thunderstorm _____

19. watching a fireworks display _____

20. waking up _____

21. running to answer a ringing telephone _____

22. hitting a home run at a baseball game _____

Standards and Benchmarks: 2A

Student Practice Sheet Two

Read the following paragraphs. Insert onomatopoeic words in the blanks to provide realistic sound effects for the various items being described. The first two have been done for you. Once you have completed your paragraphs, get a friend or relative to read your story aloud while you create the sound effects.

Sam turned the key in the lock and opened the old door to his house. **Creak!** The house was dark and quiet, as it always was when he came home from school. The **tick-tock** of the grandfather clock in the foyer seemed to echo in the large, empty house. _____ went Sam's feet as he walked into the kitchen and got the bag of potato chips that his mother had left on the counter for him. _____ went the bag as he opened it. As he ate the chips with a _____, _____, _____, he wondered what he was going to do with his afternoon. His mother had asked him to fix the leaky faucet. He could hear the _____ of the faucet now. But he didn't feel like spending his afternoon under the sink. Sam was feeling lazy, like he didn't really want to do anything. _____.

Sam turned when he heard a faint sound near the door. He looked out the sliding glass door. A small blue bird was lying on the patio. It _____ again. Sam rushed outside, ignoring the _____ sound of his stocking feet breaking through a layer of icy snow. The bird seemed to be hurt, but it still made a cheerful _____ when Sam gently picked it up. Sam carried the bird into the house, talking to him in a voice just barely above a _____. His socks made little wet puddles and _____ as he walked across the floor. Sam wasn't sure what to do for the bird. He could tell its wing was broken. Sam was starting to feel anxious, worried that the bird might die. Then he heard his mother's car pull into the driveway. _____! "Don't worry," he said to the little bird in a soothing _____. "Mom's a veterinarian. She'll know how to help you."

Standards and Benchmarks: 2A

Group Storytelling Worksheet

When you hear the boldfaced words read aloud, make the following sound effects.

Sound Effects

steps, stairs, stairway, stairwell, footsteps—March your feet.

haunted house—Say "Eeeeee!"

doorbell—Say "ding dong."

door, opening box—Say "creak."

wind—Whistle.

clock—Say "tick-tock."

ghost—Say "Ooooooh!"

heart—Say "lub-dub, lub-dub."

cat—Say "hissssss."

scurrying, rats—Run your fingertips across your desk.

The Haunted House

It was Halloween, and Jeannie wanted to do something different this year. Now that she was in the fifth grade, she was tired of the same old trick-or-treats. She wanted to do something more grown-up, more sophisticated. Her older brother had always told her stories about the old gray house up on the hill. No one lived there anymore, and her brother said it was haunted. Jeannie thought this would be just the adventure she was looking for.

Jeannie walked slowly up the **steps** of the old, gray house. She wasn't sure if she wanted to go to the **haunted house** alone, but her brother had refused to come along. As she pressed the **doorbell**, Jeannie gulped. She tried to gather all of her courage. Something about the place gave her the creeps. "Maybe my brother was right after all," she thought. "I can't go back now, though. He'll call me a chicken. Besides, who really believes in **haunted houses** anyway?" she asked herself.

Jeannie jumped as the **door** opened by itself. "Welcome to my house," boomed a loud voice. Jeannie looked around, but she couldn't see where the voice was coming from. She was the only person standing in the large, dark hallway. The curtains flew as a strong **wind** whistled through the hall. She jumped as a tall grandfather **clock** began to chime the hour. Jeannie's eyes darted towards the **door**, wondering if she should make a quick getaway.

Group Storytelling Worksheet *(cont.)*

The Haunted House *(cont.)*

When Jeannie looked back, she saw a **ghost** who gestured for her to follow him. Jeannie was puzzled by the **ghost's** presence. She was sure that he must be a person dressed in a long, white sheet, so she decided to follow it. When they turned the corner, the **ghost** began to walk up a long **stairway**. Jeannie heard her feet echoing in the empty **stairwell**. The sound frightened her. She was trying to walk softly when she realized that she was only hearing one set of **footsteps**. With an uneasy feeling, she looked toward the bottom of the ghost and saw that there weren't any feet coming out from under the bottom of the sheet. The **ghost** was really floating.

Jeannie's **heart** seemed to jump into her throat. She turned to run down the **steps** and stepped onto the tail of a **cat**. The **cat** began to claw her, forcing her to run back up the **steps** after the **ghost**. Desperate to escape the **cat**, Jeannie followed the **ghost** through the door at the top of the **stairs**.

The room was dark and gloomy. Jeannie could hardly see and immediately walked straight into a cobweb. The thin, moist strands of web clung to her face and hair. She heard a loud **scurrying** noise on the floor and looked down to see what was making the noise. The cobwebs had left her temporarily blinded and at first she could not see the hundreds of large, gray **rats** that were **scurrying** back and forth across the floor.

"Help! Help!" a voice called from inside of a wooden box. Jeannie was hesitant, but the voice sounded like that of a young girl. She wondered if it belonged to the last child who had entered the **haunted house**. The box **creaked** as she opened the top. Long white arms tried to pull Jeannie into the box. Jeannie screamed as she tried to pull herself away from the **ghost**. Her **heart** pounded loudly as she pulled and pulled. Finally she escaped from the arms and fell backward onto the **rat**-covered floor.

Jeannie immediately scrambled to her feet and rushed to the door. She ran down the **steps**, jumping over the **cat** that was waiting for her return. She heard the **doorbell** ringing as she ran through the front hall, past the **clock** and through the front **door**. "Go home!" she screamed to a child who was waiting to enter the **haunted house**. But her voice was lost in the **wind**.

Hyperbole
Teaching Guide

Goal: The students will use hyperbole to enhance their descriptive writing.

Introducing the Skill

Preparation: Reproduce the Student Resource Sheet (page 86) for students and make a copy for yourself to use as a teaching reference.

Directions: Distribute the Student Resource Sheet to students. Tell students WHAT skill they will be learning. Explain WHY writers use this skill and WHY it will make your students' writing better. Show several examples of WHEN this skill is used. Teach students HOW to use this skill.

Practicing the Skill

Preparation: Reproduce the Student Practice Sheets (pages 87 and 88) for students.

Directions: Assign the practice sheets to students according to their needs and abilities. You may wish to have students work on these sheets in one or more of the following ways: as a whole-class activity, with a partner, in small groups, or independently. As an alternative, you may prefer to use one or both sheets as homework assignments. Provide feedback to students to ensure mastery of the skill.

Applying the Skill

Preparation: None

Directions: Review that a hyperbole is a humorous exaggeration. Tell students that they are going to have a Hyperbole Hoe-Down. Explain that in this contest students will use hyperbole to create the most outrageous, absurd endings to statements you provide. Divide the class into three groups. Two groups will be teams of players. The third group will be judges. Have one player from each of the two teams go "head to head" in the Hyperbole Hoe-Down. Provide the beginning of a statement. See the Teacher Resource Sheet (page 89) for suggestions. Allow 15–30 seconds for the students (one from each team) to think of the most exaggerated, absurd ending they can. After 15–30 seconds, call time and have each student complete the statement using a hyperbole. After the two students have given their hyperbole, give the judges 15 seconds to determine which student's hyperbole was better. The winning student is the one who gets the majority of the votes among the judges. In the event of a tie among the judges, you may wish to have each of the two players come up with an alternate ending for the same beginning statement, or you can provide a new beginning statement. Continue in this manner until all players on both teams have had a turn. You may repeat the contest as often as you wish to allow each group of students to be players as well as judges.

Student Resource Sheet

What: Good writers use hyperbole to create humorous exaggeration.

Why: Good writers use hyperbole to help the reader understand the extent of an emotion, or action, or description. A hyperbole is not intended to be taken literally; it provides an exaggeration that adds to the effect of descriptive writing.

When: Writers can use hyperbole any time they are writing a description that is not intended to be totally serious. Hyperbole can be placed anywhere in a sentence.

How: Create hyperbole by stretching your imagination and avoiding common comparisons. Use hyperbole, or extreme exaggeration, to enhance a description.

Here are some examples.

She was so quiet.
She was so quiet **I wondered if she even had a tongue.**

After exercising, John's face was red.
After exercising, John's face was so red **I thought he might be from another planet.**

He has spiky, brown hair.
His hair is so spiky **you'd think he was part porcupine.**

The children moved from place to place excitedly in their preschool classroom.
The children buzzed around their classroom so excitedly **I thought they were bees looking for pollen.**

She walked gracefully down the stairs in the fashion show.
She walked so gracefully in the fashion show that **you would have thought she was floating on clouds**.

The stars lit up the night.
The stars lit up the night **like 100-watt lightbulbs in a darkened room.**

Remember, a hyperbole is figurative language. It is not intended to make the reader think that, for example, that the woman who is quiet really doesn't have a tongue or the boy with spiky hair really is a porcupine. A hyperbole adds description to help the reader visualize something.

Standards and Benchmarks: 2A

Student Practice Sheet

Read the following examples of hyperbole. In the boxes provided below and on page 88, draw a picture to illustrate each exaggerated statement.

"You must have a million candy wrappers on your bedroom floor!"

The car sped away, traveling faster than lightning.

She cried an ocean of tears.

Standards and Benchmarks: 2A

Student Practice Sheet *(cont.)*

He was so tall that his head touched the clouds.

The pavement was as hot as a frying pan.

That snake must be a hundred feet long.

Teacher Resource Sheet

Note: For use with the Hyperbole Hoe-Down.

Have students complete each statement using a hyperbole.

Here is an example. ***He was so skinny that we could see through him if we held him up to the light.***

1. He was so tall that _____.

2. She was so pretty that _____.

3. The monkey was so silly that _____.

4. I ate my breakfast faster than _____.

5. I ran faster than _____.

6. The wind blew so hard that _____.

7. My dad was so angry that _____.

8. The turtle moved so slowly that _____.

9. He was so skinny that _____.

10. There are so many blueberries in these muffins that _____.

11. The mountain was so tall that _____.

12. The ice was so slippery that _____.

13. Her vision was so bad that _____.

14. The baby cried so much that _____.

15. The water was so deep that _____.

16. I tried to do my homework, but _____.

17. I wanted to clean my room, but _____.

18. I'm so tired that _____.

19. She was so excited that _____.

20. The cat grew so quickly that _____.

21. The magician was so powerful that _____.

22. The pancakes were so big that _____.

23. The pizza was so cheesy that _____.

24. It snowed so much that _____.

25. It was so hot that _____.

26. My shoes were so tight that _____.

27. My hair was so frizzy that _____.

28. I sneezed so many times that _____.

29. I laughed so hard that _____.

30. I was so scared that _____.

Sensory Words

Note: This organizer works best with the Mini-Event Description (page 112), First Bite Description (page 118), Holiday Description (page 121), Animal Description (page 139), and Vacation Spot Description (page 142).

Use the following graphic organizer to help you generate sensory words for your writing assignment.

Write your topic here: _____

👁 **Sight Words** 👁

👂 **Sound Words** 👂

✋ **Touch Words** ✋

👃 **Smell Words** 👃

👄 **Taste Words** 👄

Attributes

Note: This organizer works best with the Block Structure Description (page 100), and the Shoe Description (page 136).

Use the following graphic organizer to help you list attributes of your subject.

The shape of my subject is best described as . . .

The size of my subject is best described as . . .

The colors of my subject are best described as . . .

Physical Description

Note: This organizer works best with the Character Sketch (page 103), Criminal Description (page 106), Face Description (page 115), and Monster Description (page 127).

Use the following graphic organizer to help you describe the physical appearance of your subject.

Name:
Height:
Weight:
Age:
Sex:
Hair color:
Eye color:
Skin color:

Distinguishing facial features:
Other distinguishing marks:
Other notable physical characteristics:
Movement:
Unique physical abilities or disabilities:

Soft Words

Note: This organizer works best with the Babysitter Report (page 97).

Use the following graphic organizer to help you describe the actions that really occurred and suggest ways to soften your description.

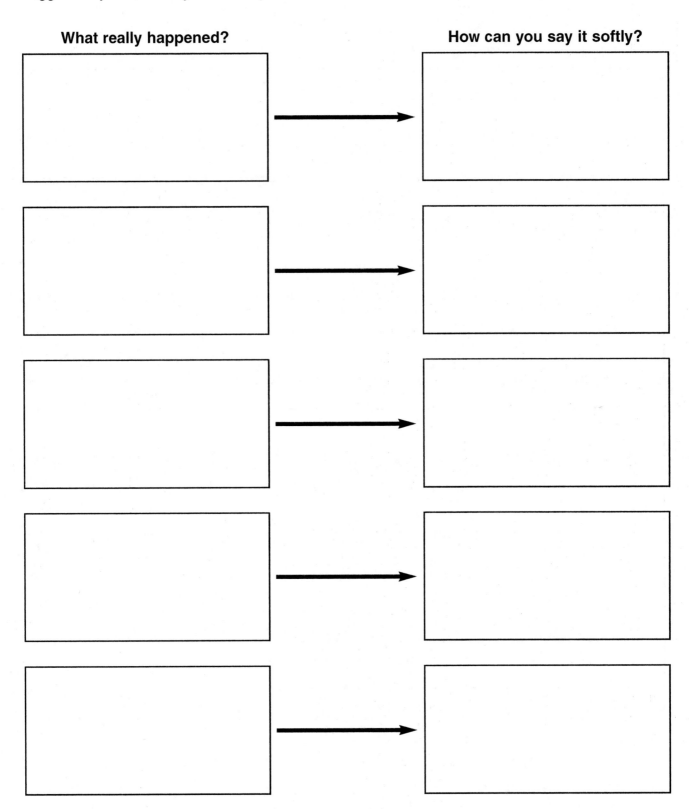

What really happened?   **How can you say it softly?**

Sequence of Steps

Note: This organizer works best with the Directions to a School Location (page 109).

Use the following graphic organizer to help you sequence directions, telling how to get from one location to another.

Positive or Negative

Note: This organizer works best with the Menu Rewrite (page 124).

Use the following graphic organizer to help you describe something in a more positive or negative manner.

First decide if you will describe the topic in a positive or negative way. Then choose your descriptive words accordingly. Select only positive or negative words, depending on your focus.

Actual Description	**Positive or Negative Words** (Circle *Positive* or *Negative* above to indicate what type of list follows.)

Blueprints

Note: This organizer works best with the Room Description (page 130).

Use the following blueprint to help you describe your room. Label the location of furniture and important objects, such as the door, windows, closets, etc. Then write descriptive words in the appropriate areas of the blueprint.

<Back>

<Floor>

<Front>

Babysitter Report

Descriptive Writing Assignment: Pretend you are babysitting for two wild, out-of-control children. You know their parents are going to ask you how they behaved. You don't really want to tell the parents how bad the children were because you want to seem in control of the situation, but you don't want to lie to the parents either. Think about how you can describe the children's behavior by "cushioning" your words a little. Think about what the children did and what they said. Decide how you can describe the children "softly" to their parents.

Because you are nervous about talking to the parents, you decide to write your report. That way you can practice your words before you speak to the parents. Write your report in a paragraph, describing the children's behavior. Be sure to include specific details, using precise word choices. Try to use sophisticated sentence structures and effective writing techniques, as appropriate. Before creating a final draft, revise and proofread your work using the checklists provided below.

Revising: When you have completed your rough draft, revise your description using the following checklist of questions.

_____ 1. Did I use the best possible word choices to describe my subject?

_____ 2. Did I use sophisticated sentence structures to enhance my description?

   (colon sentences, semicolon sentences, commas in a series, appositives, transitions, etc.)

_____ 3. Did I use effective writing techniques to enhance my description?

   (similes, metaphors, personification, onomatopoeia, hyperbole, etc.)

_____ 4. Did I include a topic sentence, detail sentences, and a concluding sentence?

_____ 5. Did I use "soft words" in my description.

Proofreading: Before you write your final draft, proofread your description using the following checklist of questions.

_____ 1. Did I capitalize the first word of each sentence?

_____ 2. Did I capitalize any proper nouns (names of people or places)?

_____ 3. Did I place correct punctuation at the end of each sentence?

_____ 4. Did I indent my paragraph?

_____ 5. Did I spell all words correctly, and did I use a dictionary to check the spelling of any words I was unsure about?

Babysitter Report *(cont.)*

Publishing and Technology Option: Instead of simply word processing your report, send it as an e-mail attachment to the fictional parents. Use the e-mail address of your school or teacher for a real address.

Home-School Connections: Invite your parents to tell you stories about when they were children and what they did when they had a babysitter. Try to come up with "cushioned" words to describe any inappropriate behavior.

Tommy and Anna certainly have healthy appetites. They each had several slices of pizza, ate all of their vegetables, and even had room for two bowls of popcorn later in the evening. We ate in front of the television, so they could watch their favorite show. Tommy insisted that their other babysitter always allowed them to watch TV all night. With some difficulty, I managed to turn off the television and persuaded them to play a game. However, they seemed to have too much energy for a board game. As a result, the pizza, which was still on the TV trays, ended up on the floor. After the unfortunate accident with the pizza, Anna got up and stormed out of the room, knocking over the lamp that was on the table. Naturally, that made her even more upset. I assured her that everyone has an occasional accident, and that seemed to make her feel better. Then Tommy began scaring her with stories of what her punishment might be for breaking the lamp. I thought it would be best for them to spend some time alone in their own bedrooms. The rest of the evening went fairly smoothly. At one point when I was building a model airplane with Tommy, I noticed that I hadn't heard anything from Anna in a little while. When I searched for her, I found her trying to beautify herself with your makeup. I'm sorry about the mess. I tried to clean it up, but I didn't know how to get the lipstick out of the bedspread. After all of the excitement, you would think that Tommy and Anna would be worn out. But, this was not the case. Eventually, I got them into bed, but only after I suggested we tell ghost stories. Tommy started scaring Anna again. That's why she's sleeping under the bed right now. They certainly are creative children.

Babysitter Report *(cont.)*

Assessment Rubric:

- Criteria for **EXCELLENT** babysitter reports

_____ The description is written in a well-developed paragraph, with cohesive topic, detail, and concluding sentences.

_____ The description evokes strong sensory images.

_____ The author uses precise word choices to depict the subject of the description.

_____ The author uses many sophisticated sentence structures to enhance the description.

(Check all those included.)

❑ colon sentences   ❑ appositives   ❑ commas in a series
❑ semicolon sentences   ❑ transitions
❑ other: _____

_____ The author uses many effective writing techniques to enhance the description.

_____ Spelling, capitalization, and punctuation are correct.

- Criteria for **SATISFACTORY** babysitter reports

_____ The description is written in a well-developed paragraph, with topic, detail, and concluding sentences.

_____ The description evokes sensory images.

_____ The author uses effective word choices to depict the subject of the description.

_____ The author uses some sophisticated sentence structures in the description.

(Check all those included.)

❑ colon sentences   ❑ appositives   ❑ commas in a series
❑ semicolon sentences   ❑ transitions
❑ other: _____

_____ The author uses some effective writing techniques to enhance the description.

_____ Spelling, capitalization, and punctuation errors do not interfere with the meaning of the description.

- Criteria for **UNSATISFACTORY** babysitter reports

_____ The description may not be written in paragraph form and may lack topic, detail, and/or concluding sentences.

_____ The description does not include sensory images.

_____ The author does not use effective word choices to depict the subject of the description.

_____ The author does not use sophisticated sentence structures in the description.

_____ The author does not use effective writing techniques to enhance the description.

_____ Spelling, capitalization, and punctuation errors interfere with the meaning of the description.

Block Structure Description

Descriptive Writing Assignment: Find some building blocks that you can use to help you with this assignment. Create a structure using the building blocks you have collected. Pretend that you are an architect, and let your imagination run wild. You can make your structure as large or as small as you wish. You are only limited by your imagination and the number of blocks you have.

When you are satisfied with your creation, write one or more paragraphs describing the appearance of your structure. Think about the following: size and shape of your structure, the colors of the blocks, the combination and types of blocks you used, and what things you could compare your structure to. Be sure to include specific details in your paragraph(s) so the reader will know exactly what your creation looks like. Try to use sophisticated sentence structures and effective writing techniques, as appropriate. Before creating a final draft, revise and proofread your work using the checklists provided below.

Revising: When you have completed your rough draft, revise your description using the following checklist of questions.

_____ 1. Did I use the best possible word choices to describe my subject?

_____ 2. Did I use sophisticated sentence structures to enhance my description?

(colon sentences, semicolon sentence, commas in a series, appositives, transitions, etc.)

_____ 3. Did I use effective writing techniques to enhance my description?

(similes, metaphors, onomatopoeia, hyperbole, etc.)

_____ 4. Did I include a topic sentence, detail sentences, and a concluding sentence?

_____ 5. Does my description allow the reader to "see" my structure?

Proofreading: Before you write your final draft, proofread your description using the following checklist of questions.

_____ 1. Did I capitalize the first word of each sentence?

_____ 2. Did I capitalize any proper nouns (names of people or places)?

_____ 3. Did I place correct punctuation at the end of each sentence?

_____ 4. Did I indent my paragraph(s)?

_____ 5. Did I spell all words correctly, and did I use a dictionary to check the spelling of any words I was unsure about?

Block Structure Description *(cont.)*

Publishing and Technology Option: Experiment with different types of fonts when word processing your description. Depending on your subject, you may wish to use flowery letters (if you created a garden), royal-looking letters (if you created a castle), childish letters (if you created a playground), etc. Be creative.

Home-School Connection: Notice how your home is designed. Talk with a family member about how you would describe your home's outside appearance.

My castle is majestic and strong. I pretend that it sits at the top of a tall mountain, overlooking the valley and the people below. The long road that leads to the castle is made up of ten rectangular blocks, each six inches (15 cm) in length. Surrounding the castle is a circular moat created with twenty blue blocks, each three inches (7.5 cm) long. There is a bridge that leads from the road to the castle. Supported by a long, rectangular block, it is layered with fifteen thin, long cylinders that create the appearance of a log bridge. The entrance to the castle is marked by hinged double doors, which are made with two red, rectangular blocks that are standing vertically. One of the doors stands open, inviting visitors to enter the castle. The outside of the castle is made from squares, with each side being twenty blocks high and fifteen blocks wide. The square blocks are placed in alternating colors of green and blue. The roof of the castle begins at the last row of alternating green and blue blocks. The first part of the roof is made with red, rectangular blocks, lying horizontally around the top of the walls. The roof is flat and made with three levels of red, rectangular blocks. A green and blue flag hangs from a pencil that is stuck in the very top of the castle. This is the flag of the kingdom.

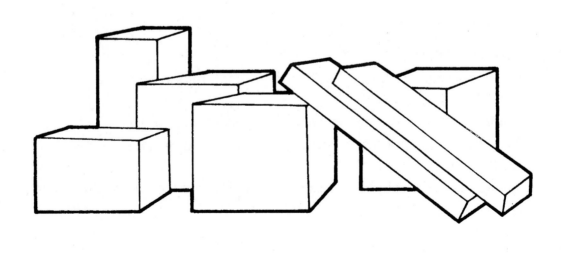

Block Structure Description *(cont.)*

Assessment Rubric:

- Criteria for **EXCELLENT** block structure descriptions

_____ The description is written in a well-developed paragraph, with cohesive topic, detail, and concluding sentences.

_____ The description evokes strong sensory images.

_____ The author uses precise word choices to depict the subject of the description.

_____ The author uses many sophisticated sentence structures to enhance the description.

(Check all those included.)

❏ colon sentences   ❏ appositives   ❏ commas in a series
❏ semicolon sentences   ❏ transitions
❏ other: _____

_____ The author uses many effective writing techniques to enhance the description.

_____ Spelling, capitalization, and punctuation are correct.

- Criteria for **SATISFACTORY** block structure descriptions

_____ The description is written in a well-developed paragraph, with topic, detail, and concluding sentences.

_____ The description evokes sensory images.

_____ The author uses effective word choices to depict the subject of the description.

_____ The author uses some sophisticated sentence structures in the description.

(Check all those included.)

❏ colon sentences   ❏ appositives   ❏ commas in a series
❏ semicolon sentences   ❏ transitions
❏ other: _____

_____ The author uses some effective writing techniques to enhance the description.

_____ Spelling, capitalization, and punctuation errors do not interfere with the meaning of the description.

- Criteria for **UNSATISFACTORY** block structure descriptions

_____ The description may not be written in paragraph form and may lack topic, detail, and/or concluding sentences.

_____ The description does not include sensory images.

_____ The author does not use effective word choices to depict the subject of the description.

_____ The author does not use sophisticated sentence structures in the description.

_____ The author does not use effective writing techniques to enhance the description.

_____ Spelling, capitalization, and punctuation errors interfere with the meaning of the description.

Character Sketch

Descriptive Writing Assignment: Sit in a location where you won't be noticed. Study the appearance and actions of a person you can see. Notice the following: the physical appearance of the person, how the person is dressed, how the person's face and hair looks, what the person is doing, and what the person might be saying or thinking.

Write a character sketch of the person you have been studying. Try to capture the "essence" of that person's character. Be sure to include specific details, using precise word choices. In addition, try to use sophisticated sentence structures and effective writing techniques, as appropriate. Before creating a final draft, revise and proofread your work using the checklists provided below.

Revising: When you have completed your rough draft, revise your description using the following checklist of questions.

_____ 1. Did I use the best possible word choices to describe my subject?

_____ 2. Did I use sophisticated sentence structures to enhance my description?

(colon sentences, semicolon sentences, commas in a series, appositives, transitions, etc.)

_____ 3. Did I use effective writing techniques to enhance my description?

(similes, metaphors, onomatopoeia, hyperbole, etc.)

_____ 4. Did I include a topic sentence, detail sentences, and a concluding sentence?

_____ 5. Does my description allow the reader to "see" the character?

Proofreading: Before you write your final draft, proofread your description using the following checklist of questions.

_____ 1. Did I capitalize the first word of each sentence?

_____ 2. Did I capitalize any proper nouns (names of people or places)?

_____ 3. Did I place correct punctuation at the end of each sentence?

_____ 4. Did I indent my paragraph(s)?

_____ 5. Did I spell all words correctly, and did I use a dictionary to check the spelling of any words I was unsure about?

Character Sketch *(cont.)*

Publishing and Technology Option: Make a collage of items that relate to the character you have studied. For example, if the person was eating in a fast-food restaurant, cut out pictures of French fries, soda, etc., and glue them onto a piece of construction paper. Write your character sketch on a piece of plain paper and glue it in the center of the collage. You may prefer to make your collage on a computer by collecting pictures from a clip art or graphics program.

Home-School Connection: Secretly study a family member. Write a character sketch, describing this person.

Martha rocks quietly with her infant son in her arms. She gazes at him with proud eyes, the eyes of a new mother. Her blue eyes sparkle and never leave her son's face. She gently brushes a strand of her wavy, chocolate hair from her face. She softly hums a lullaby, "Go to sleep, and good-night. . ." Her baby coos and shifts in her arms. Martha's feet continue to move the rocker gently back and forth, back and forth. A soft, blue blanket is draped over her legs, keeping both her and the baby warm in the middle of a cool night. Soon the baby is fast asleep, but Martha continues to rock and sing.

Character Sketch *(cont.)*

Assessment Rubric:

- Criteria for **EXCELLENT** character descriptions

_____ The description is written in a well-developed paragraph, with cohesive topic, detail, and concluding sentences.

_____ The description evokes strong sensory images.

_____ The author uses precise word choices to depict the subject of the description.

_____ The author uses many sophisticated sentence structures to enhance the description.

(Check all those included.)

❑ colon sentences ❑ appositives ❑ commas in a series
❑ semicolon sentences ❑ transitions
❑ other: _____

_____ The author uses many effective writing techniques to enhance the description.

_____ Spelling, capitalization, and punctuation are correct.

- Criteria for **SATISFACTORY** character descriptions

_____ The description is written in a well-developed paragraph, with topic, detail, and concluding sentences.

_____ The description evokes sensory images.

_____ The author uses effective word choices to depict the subject of the description.

_____ The author uses some sophisticated sentence structures in the description.

(Check all those included.)

❑ colon sentences ❑ appositives ❑ commas in a series
❑ semicolon sentences ❑ transitions
❑ other: _____

_____ The author uses some effective writing techniques to enhance the description.

_____ Spelling, capitalization, and punctuation errors do not interfere with the meaning of the description.

- Criteria for **UNSATISFACTORY** character descriptions

_____ The description may not be written in paragraph form and may lack topic, detail, and/or concluding sentences.

_____ The description does not include sensory images.

_____ The author does not use effective word choices to depict the subject of the description.

_____ The author does not use sophisticated sentence structures in the description.

_____ The author does not use effective writing techniques to enhance the description.

_____ Spelling, capitalization, and punctuation errors interfere with the meaning of the description.

Standards and Benchmarks: 1A 1B, 1C, 1E, 1F, 2A, 2B, 2C, 3B, 3C, 3D, 3E, 3F, 3G, 3H, 3J, 3K, 3L

Criminal Description

Descriptive Writing Assignment: Pretend you have witnessed a crime and the police have asked you to describe the appearance of the criminal for their wanted poster. Think about the following aspects: what the criminal looked like (including the criminal's approximate age, height, and weight; facial features; hair color and style; distinguishing marks such as scars, tattoos, etc.), whether the criminal was male or female, and what the criminal was wearing.

Write a paragraph for the police, describing the appearance of the criminal for their wanted poster. Be sure to include specific details, using precise word choices. Try to use sophisticated sentence structures and effective writing techniques, as appropriate. Before creating a final draft, revise and proofread your work using the checklists provided below.

Revising: When you have completed your rough draft, revise your description using the following checklist of questions.

_____ 1. Did I use the best possible word choices to describe my subject?

_____ 2. Did I use sophisticated sentence structures to enhance my description?

(colon sentences, semicolon sentences, commas in a series, appositives, transitions, etc.)

_____ 3. Did I use effective writing techniques to enhance my description?

(similes, metaphors, onomatopoeia, hyperbole, etc.)

_____ 4. Did I include a topic sentence, detail sentences, and a concluding sentence?

_____ 5. Does my description allow the reader to "see" the criminal?

Proofreading: Before you write your final draft, proofread your description using the following checklist of questions.

_____ 1. Did I capitalize the first word of each sentence?

_____ 2. Did I capitalize any proper nouns (names of people or places)?

_____ 3. Did I place correct punctuation at the end of each sentence?

_____ 4. Did I indent my paragraph?

_____ 5. Did I spell all words correctly, and did I use a dictionary to check the spelling of any words I was unsure about?

Criminal Description *(cont.)*

Publishing and Technology Option: Design a wanted poster to accompany your description. Draw a picture of the criminal you have described and attach it to your description. You could even use a drawing program on the computer to create your criminal's face.

Home-School Connection: Design a humorous wanted poster for a member of your family who has committed a "household crime" such as using up all of the toilet paper or leaving dirty clothes on the floor.

The criminal was a male who appeared to be between 20 and 25 years of age. He was approximately five feet ten inches (175 cm) tall. His brown, curly hair was long, with several shocking streaks of white-blond in it. His hair covered most of his forehead, but it was thin enough that I could see the dark red scar on the top of his forehead. His face was square and very pale, as if he had not been outside in quite a while. His bushy, dark eyebrows stood out clearly from his pale face. The huge, green eyes were his most notable feature. Streaked with flecks of gold, his piercing eyes were framed by long, golden lashes. His nose was long and thin, with freckles across the bridge. Next to his nose he had a small, dark mark that looked like a birthmark. He had another birthmark on his arm, right underneath a large tattoo. Although I could tell the tattoo was a python, it did not look like a professional tattoo. I could easily see the tattoo because he was wearing a short-sleeved, gray T-shirt. The shirt looked old because the collar was worn and the material was very thin, as if it had been washed many times.

Criminal Description *(cont.)*

Assessment Rubric:

- Criteria for **EXCELLENT** criminal descriptions

_____ The description is written in a well-developed paragraph, with cohesive topic, detail, and concluding sentences.

_____ The description evokes strong sensory images.

_____ The author uses precise word choices to depict the subject of the description.

_____ The author uses many sophisticated sentence structures to enhance the description.

(Check all those included.)

❑ colon sentences   ❑ appositives   ❑ commas in a series
❑ semicolon sentences   ❑ transitions
❑ other: _____

_____ The author uses many effective writing techniques to enhance the description.

_____ Spelling, capitalization, and punctuation are correct.

- Criteria for **SATISFACTORY** criminal descriptions

_____ The description is written in a well-developed paragraph, with topic, detail, and concluding sentences.

_____ The description evokes sensory images.

_____ The author uses effective word choices to depict the subject of the description.

_____ The author uses some sophisticated sentence structures in the description.

(Check all those included.)

❑ colon sentences   ❑ appositives   ❑ commas in a series
❑ semicolon sentences   ❑ transitions
❑ other: _____

_____ The author uses some effective writing techniques to enhance the description.

_____ Spelling, capitalization, and punctuation errors do not interfere with the meaning of the description.

- Criteria for **UNSATISFACTORY** criminal descriptions

_____ The description may not be written in paragraph form and may lack topic, detail, and/or concluding sentences.

_____ The description does not include sensory images.

_____ The author does not use effective word choices to depict the subject of the description.

_____ The author does not use sophisticated sentence structures in the description.

_____ The author does not use effective writing techniques to enhance the description.

_____ Spelling, capitalization, and punctuation errors interfere with the meaning of the description.

Directions to a School Location

Descriptive Writing Assignment: Pretend that you have a new student in your class, and your teacher has asked you to write directions to a specific location in the school for this new student.

Choose one of the following locations:

— cafeteria	— nearest boy's bathroom	— main office
— nearest water fountain	— music room	— teachers' lounge
— nearest girl's bathroom	— counselor's office	— nurse's office
— gymnasium	— art room	— the stage

Write clear directions from your classroom to the location you have selected. Think about: what you do when you exit your classroom door, the turns involved, the "landmarks" along the way, and the length of time it should take to arrive at the destination.

Write a paragraph giving directions from your classroom to a specific location in your school. Be sure to include specific details, using precise word choices. Try to use sophisticated sentence structures and effective writing techniques, as appropriate. Before creating a final draft, revise and proofread your work using the checklists provided below.

Revising: When you have completed your rough draft, revise your description using the following checklist of questions.

_____ 1. Did I use the best possible word choices to describe my subject?

_____ 2. Did I use sophisticated sentence structures to enhance my description?

(colon sentences, semicolon sentences, commas in a series, appositives, transitions, etc.)

_____ 3. Did I use effective writing techniques to enhance my description?

(similes, metaphors, onomatopoeia, hyperbole, etc.)

_____ 4. Did I include a topic sentence, detail sentences, and a concluding sentence?

_____ 5. Using my directions, will the student find the location?

Proofreading: Before you write your final draft, proofread your description using the following checklist of questions.

_____ 1. Did I capitalize the first word of each sentence?

_____ 2. Did I capitalize any proper nouns (names of people or places)?

_____ 3. Did I place correct punctuation at the end of each sentence?

_____ 4. Did I indent my paragraph?

_____ 5. Did I spell all words correctly, and did I use a dictionary to check the spelling of any words I was unsure about?

Directions to a School Location *(cont.)*

Publishing and Technology Option: Draw or use a drawing program on a computer to create a map to go with your directions.

Home-School Connection: Write directions from your bedroom to another room in your house. Have a family member start at your bedroom and try to follow your directions. See if this family member ends up where you intended.

Turn right as you walk out of our classroom. Follow the red lockers, passing the third-grade classrooms, until you reach a set of doors. Go through those doors, and walk forward two steps. Do not go through the next door. You will see a set of stairs on your right. Follow those stairs up one level. There is a door at the top, but you should not go through this door either. Instead, follow the stairs up one more level. Go straight. Pass a long row of yellow lockers and then blue lockers. Go through the door on the right to enter the cafeteria. Walk to the other side of the cafeteria. There will be two doors on that side of the cafeteria. You want to go through the door on the left. As you walk out of the cafeteria, the first thing you will notice is the boys' bathroom on your left. Then you will pass the water fountain, followed by the girls' bathroom. Now you are in the main lobby. The office is on the right-hand side, surrounded by glass windows. It looks like an aquarium, but it doesn't have any fish. When you walk into the office, try to find the secretary with the short, brown, curly hair. She is usually working at the front desk. If she is not there, check the first desk on the left. If you get lost along the way, just ask someone for help.

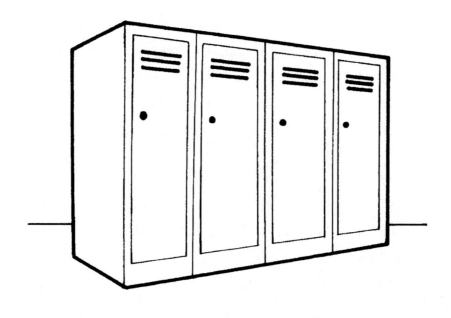

Directions to a School Location *(cont.)*

Assessment Rubric:

- Criteria for **EXCELLENT** directions

_____ The description is written in a well-developed paragraph, with cohesive topic, detail, and concluding sentences.

_____ The description evokes strong sensory images.

_____ The author uses precise word choices to depict the subject of the description.

_____ The author uses many sophisticated sentence structures to enhance the description.

(Check all those included.)

❏ colon sentences ❏ appositives ❏ commas in a series
❏ semicolon sentences ❏ transitions
❏ other: _____

_____ The author uses many effective writing techniques to enhance the description.

_____ Spelling, capitalization, and punctuation are correct.

- Criteria for **SATISFACTORY** directions

_____ The description is written in a well-developed paragraph, with topic, detail, and concluding sentences.

_____ The description evokes sensory images.

_____ The author uses effective word choices to depict the subject of the description.

_____ The author uses some sophisticated sentence structures in the description.

(Check all those included.)

❏ colon sentences ❏ appositives ❏ commas in a series
❏ semicolon sentences ❏ transitions
❏ other: _____

_____ The author uses some effective writing techniques to enhance the description.

_____ Spelling, capitalization, and punctuation errors do not interfere with the meaning of the description.

- Criteria for **UNSATISFACTORY** directions

_____ The description may not be written in paragraph form and may lack topic, detail, and/or concluding sentences.

_____ The description does not include sensory images.

_____ The author does not use effective word choices to depict the subject of the description.

_____ The author does not use sophisticated sentence structures in the description.

_____ The author does not use effective writing techniques to enhance the description.

_____ Spelling, capitalization, and punctuation errors interfere with the meaning of the description.

Mini-Event Description

Descriptive Writing Assignment: Use your knowledge of descriptive writing techniques to describe a mini-event. Choose from the list of mini-events below or think of one of your own that would be similar to those suggested.

— a thunderstorm	— surfing on a big wave and then being wiped out
— leaves falling from a tree	— a pitcher throwing a 90 mile-per-hour fastball
— raking leaves into a pile	— the "wave" in a crowded stadium
— a fire in the fireplace	— bacon frying in a pan
— walking in the park	— roasting marshmallows
— blowing out candles	— an automatic car wash
— bungee jumping	— shoveling snow off a sidewalk

Think about the following: what happens at the beginning of the mini-event; what specific sights, sounds, smells, tastes, and textures are associated with different stages of the mini-event; how the mini-event progresses; and what happens at the end of the mini-event.

Write a paragraph describing the sequence of your mini-event. Be sure to include specific details, using precise word choices. Try to use sophisticated sentence structures and effective writing techniques, as appropriate. Before creating a final draft, revise and proofread your work using the checklist provided below and on page 113.

Revising: When you have completed your rough draft, revise your description using the following checklist of questions.

_____ 1. Did I use the best possible word choices to describe my subject?

_____ 2. Did I use sophisticated sentence structures to enhance my description?

(colon sentences, semicolon sentences, commas in a series, appositives, transitions, etc.)

_____ 3. Did I use effective writing techniques to enhance my description?

(similes, metaphors, onomatopoeia, hyperbole, etc.)

_____ 4. Did I include a topic sentence, detail sentences, and a concluding sentence?

_____ 5. Will my description allow the reader to "experience" my mini-event?

Mini-Event Description *(cont.)*

Proofreading: Before you write your final draft, proofread your description using the following checklist of questions.

_____ 1. Did I capitalize the first word of each sentence?

_____ 2. Did I capitalize any proper nouns (names of people or places)?

_____ 3. Did I place correct punctuation at the end of each sentence?

_____ 4. Did I indent my paragraph?

_____ 5. Did I spell all words correctly, and did I use a dictionary to check the spelling of any words I was unsure about?

Publishing and Technology Option: Use a graphics program on a computer to import a picture of your subject. You could use the picture as a watermark, which is a faint outline behind your text, for an interesting effect.

Home-School Connection: Read your description to a family member. Ask that person to close his or her eyes and picture the mini-event as you read your description. When you have finished, talk about what your family member pictured.

The man sighs as another match dies out before the fire gets started. He adds a handful of twigs to the fire that ignites instantly. The man stands back to watch the fire grow. Flames rise from the twigs in bright orange streaks, touching the logs that rest directly above them. The twigs fall apart and turn to ash as the flames reach the logs above. The flames lick the logs hungrily, spreading from side to side throughout the fire. The fire reaches high into the sky, covering the logs with flames. The man looks and smiles when he sees the logs glowing with fire. The man sits and relaxes by the warm, crackling fire. Waves of flickering sparks jump over the thick logs, reflecting in the man's eyes. The crackling and burning sounds seem to echo in the quiet forest. Frenzied flashes of vibrant colors dance over the charred wood. In time, this will all be a smoldering pile of ashes.

Mini-Event Description *(cont.)*

Assessment Rubric:

- Criteria for **EXCELLENT** mini-event descriptions

_____ The description is written in a well-developed paragraph, with cohesive topic, detail, and concluding sentences.

_____ The description evokes strong sensory images.

_____ The author uses precise word choices to depict the subject of the description.

_____ The author uses many sophisticated sentence structures to enhance the description.

(Check all those included.)

❏ colon sentences   ❏ appositives   ❏ commas in a series
❏ semicolon sentences   ❏ transitions
❏ other: _____

_____ The author uses many effective writing techniques to enhance the description.

_____ Spelling, capitalization, and punctuation are correct.

- Criteria for **SATISFACTORY** mini-event descriptions

_____ The description is written in a well-developed paragraph, with topic, detail, and concluding sentences.

_____ The description evokes sensory images.

_____ The author uses effective word choices to depict the subject of the description.

_____ The author uses some sophisticated sentence structures in the description.

(Check all those included.)

❏ colon sentences   ❏ appositives   ❏ commas in a series
❏ semicolon sentences   ❏ transitions
❏ other: _____

_____ The author uses some effective writing techniques to enhance the description.

_____ Spelling, capitalization, and punctuation errors do not interfere with the meaning of the description.

- Criteria for **UNSATISFACTORY** mini-event descriptions

_____ The description may not be written in paragraph form and may lack topic, detail, and/or concluding sentences.

_____ The description does not include sensory images.

_____ The author does not use effective word choices to depict the subject of the description.

_____ The author does not use sophisticated sentence structures in the description.

_____ The author does not use effective writing techniques to enhance the description.

_____ Spelling, capitalization, and punctuation errors interfere with the meaning of the description.

Face Description

Descriptive Writing Assignment: Think of a person you find attractive. This person could be someone famous, like a singer, an actor, a model, or it could be someone you know like a relative or friend. Think about the following: the person's face, eyes, nose, mouth, hair, and skin tone.

Write one or two paragraphs describing the appearance of this person's face. Be sure to include specific details, using precise word choices. Try to use sophisticated sentence structures and effective writing techniques, as appropriate. Before creating a final draft, revise and proofread your work using the checklists provided below.

Revising: When you have completed your rough draft, revise your description using the following checklist of questions.

_____ 1. Did I use the best possible word choices to describe my subject?

_____ 2. Did I use sophisticated sentence structures to enhance my description?

(colon sentences, semicolon sentences, commas in a series, appositives, transitions, etc.)

_____ 3. Did I use effective writing techniques to enhance my description?

(similes, metaphors, onomatopoeia, hyperbole, etc.)

_____ 4. Did I include a topic sentence, detail sentences, and a concluding sentence?

_____ 5. Does my description allow the reader to "see" this person?

Proofreading: Before you write your final draft, proofread your description using the following checklist of questions.

_____ 1. Did I capitalize the first word of each sentence?

_____ 2. Did I capitalize any proper nouns (names of people or places)?

_____ 3. Did I place correct punctuation at the end of each sentence?

_____ 4. Did I indent my paragraph(s)?

_____ 5. Did I spell all words correctly, and did I use a dictionary to check the spelling of any words I was unsure about?

Face Description *(cont.)*

Publishing and Technology Option: Scan a picture of your subject into a computer. Export the picture to your word processing program. Print the picture along with your description.

Home-School Connection: Write a description of a family member's face.

Meet Pierre. A champion surfer at Malibu Beach, Pierre is simply captivating. His wavy, coal-black hair frames his sun-bronzed face. The ripples in his hair mirror the ripples of the water as he skillfully rides wave after wave to the shore. His hazel-green eyes, dotted with flecks of golden brown, sparkle in the sunlight. The eyelashes that frame his eyes are soft and long. Pierre's full lips are ruby red and moist. Beneath those lips are straight, pearly-white teeth. His nose is long and distinguished-looking. On the right side of his nose lies the pale white line of a scar. This scar is invisible to most, noticed only by those who stand close to Pierre.

When surrounded by adoring fans, Pierre often begins to chew anxiously on his lip. His eyes shift from one side to the other, almost as if he is looking for a way to escape from the crowd. The muscles in his face are tense, making him look nervous, even scared. Pierre's face appears relaxed and calm only when he is in the water, riding the waves on his long, black surfboard.

Face Description *(cont.)*

Assessment Rubric:

- Criteria for **EXCELLENT** face descriptions

_____ The description is written in a well-developed paragraph, with cohesive topic, detail, and concluding sentences.

_____ The description evokes strong sensory images.

_____ The author uses precise word choices to depict the subject of the description.

_____ The author uses many sophisticated sentence structures to enhance the description.

(Check all those included.)

❏ colon sentences ❏ appositives ❏ commas in a series
❏ semicolon sentences ❏ transitions
❏ other: _____

_____ The author uses many effective writing techniques to enhance the description.

_____ Spelling, capitalization, and punctuation are correct.

- Criteria for **SATISFACTORY** face descriptions

_____ The description is written in a well-developed paragraph, with topic, detail, and concluding sentences.

_____ The description evokes sensory images.

_____ The author uses effective word choices to depict the subject of the description.

_____ The author uses some sophisticated sentence structures in the description.

(Check all those included.)

❏ colon sentences ❏ appositives ❏ commas in a series
❏ semicolon sentences ❏ transitions
❏ other: _____

_____ The author uses some effective writing techniques to enhance the description.

_____ Spelling, capitalization, and punctuation errors do not interfere with the meaning of the description.

- Criteria for **UNSATISFACTORY** face descriptions

_____ The description may not be written in paragraph form and may lack topic, detail, and/or concluding sentences.

_____ The description does not include sensory images.

_____ The author does not use effective word choices to depict the subject of the description.

_____ The author does not use sophisticated sentence structures in the description.

_____ The author does not use effective writing techniques to enhance the description.

_____ Spelling, capitalization, and punctuation errors interfere with the meaning of the description.

First Bite Description

Descriptive Writing Assignment: Take a bite of your favorite food. Don't swallow it right away. Savor the flavor. Think about the following: how the food smells, the texture of the food in your mouth, and how the food changes in taste and texture as you chew it.

Write a paragraph describing the taste of your favorite food. Be sure to include specific details, using precise word choices. Try to use sophisticated sentence structures and effective writing techniques, as appropriate. Before creating a final draft, revise and proofread your work using the checklists provided below.

Revising: When you have completed your rough draft, revise your description using the following checklist of questions.

_____ 1. Did I use the best possible word choices to describe my subject?

_____ 2. Did I use sophisticated sentence structures to enhance my description?

(colon sentences, semicolon sentences, commas in a series, appositives, transitions, etc.)

_____ 3. Did I use effective writing techniques to enhance my description?

(similes, metaphors, onomatopoeia, hyperbole, etc.)

_____ 4. Did I include a topic sentence, detail sentences, and a concluding sentence?

_____ 5. Does my description allow the reader to "taste" my favorite food?

Proofreading: Before you write your final draft, proofread your description using the following checklist of questions.

_____ 1. Did I capitalize the first word of each sentence?

_____ 2. Did I capitalize any proper nouns (names of people or places)?

_____ 3. Did I place correct punctuation at the end of each sentence?

_____ 4. Did I indent my paragraph(s)?

_____ 5. Did I spell all words correctly, and did I use a dictionary to check the spelling of any words I was unsure about?

First Bite Description *(cont.)*

Publishing and Technology Option: Use a word processing program on a computer to type the final draft of your description. Use the font features to change your sensory words to boldface or italics so they stand out for the reader.

Home-School Connection: Take a bite of your dinner. Write a brief description as you enjoy the first bite. After you have swallowed the food, read your description for your family. The cook in the family will most certainly appreciate it.

My mouth is salivating as we approach Barton's Ice Cream Store. It has been ages since I have eaten an ice cream cone, and I am so excited I can almost taste the cool sweetness on my tongue. As we enter the store, my nose is filled with sweet smells of the ice cream. The list of flavors is huge, almost overwhelming. As my eyes read the names of every flavor, my mouth imagines the taste of each one. Black cherry is delicious, each mouthful a sweet cherry taste combined with the crunch of fresh fruit. Butter crunch is another one of my favorites. I love the rich, buttery taste accented by crunchy nuggets. My stomach begins to growl, impatient with my inability to decide on just one flavor. Finally I decide to get two scoops of ice cream: raspberry with vanilla on top. As the clerk starts to hand me the cone stacked with two scoops of ice cream, I ask her to please roll the cone in rainbow sprinkles. At last the clerk passes the completed cone to me. The first bite is perfect. I hold the mouthful of ice cream on my tongue for a moment, savoring the cold temperature and creamy flavor before I crunch the rainbow sprinkles. Each sprinkle seems to have its own fruity flavor. The flavor of the sprinkles is gone quickly. However, the dreamy, creamy vanilla ice cream takes over. I roll the cold sweetness around in my mouth. The cold chills my cheeks, tongue, teeth, and throat. The light, airy sweetness disappears too quickly, so I bring the cone to my lips again, eager for the next delicious bite.

First Bite Description *(cont.)*

Assessment Rubric:

- Criteria for **EXCELLENT** first bite descriptions

_____ The description is written in a well-developed paragraph, with cohesive topic, detail, and concluding sentences.

_____ The description evokes strong sensory images.

_____ The author uses precise word choices to depict the subject of the description.

_____ The author uses many sophisticated sentence structures to enhance the description.

(Check all those included.)

❑ colon sentences   ❑ appositives   ❑ commas in a series
❑ semicolon sentences   ❑ transitions
❑ other: _____

_____ The author uses many effective writing techniques to enhance the description.

_____ Spelling, capitalization, and punctuation are correct.

- Criteria for **SATISFACTORY** first bite descriptions

_____ The description is written in a well-developed paragraph, with topic, detail, and concluding sentences.

_____ The description evokes sensory images.

_____ The author uses effective word choices to depict the subject of the description.

_____ The author uses some sophisticated sentence structures in the description.

(Check all those included.)

❑ colon sentences   ❑ appositives   ❑ commas in a series
❑ semicolon sentences   ❑ transitions
❑ other: _____

_____ The author uses some effective writing techniques to enhance the description.

_____ Spelling, capitalization, and punctuation errors do not interfere with the meaning of the description.

- Criteria for **UNSATISFACTORY** first bite descriptions

_____ The description may not be written in paragraph form and may lack topic, detail, and/or concluding sentences.

_____ The description does not include sensory images.

_____ The author does not use effective word choices to depict the subject of the description.

_____ The author does not use sophisticated sentence structures in the description.

_____ The author does not use effective writing techniques to enhance the description.

_____ Spelling, capitalization, and punctuation errors interfere with the meaning of the description.

Holiday Description

Descriptive Writing Assignment: Pick your favorite holiday. Then think about the following: how you celebrate that holiday (what you do and any traditions you follow related to that holiday), what you see on that holiday, what smells are associated with that holiday, and how you feel on that holiday.

Write a paragraph describing your favorite holiday. Be sure to include specific details, using precise word choices. Try to use sophisticated sentence structures and effective writing techniques, as appropriate. Before creating a final draft, revise and proofread your work using the checklist provided below.

Revising: When you have completed your rough draft, revise your description using the following checklist of questions.

_____ 1. Did I use the best possible word choices to describe my subject?

_____ 2. Did I use sophisticated sentence structures to enhance my description?

(colon sentences, semicolon sentences, commas in a series, appositives, transitions, etc.)

_____ 3. Did I use effective writing techniques to enhance my description?

(similes, metaphors, onomatopoeia, hyperbole, etc.)

_____ 4. Did I include a topic sentence, detail sentences, and a concluding sentence?

_____ 5. Does my description allow the reader to "experience" the holiday?

Proofreading: Before you write your final draft, proofread your description using the following checklist of questions.

_____ 1. Did I capitalize the first word of each sentence?

_____ 2. Did I capitalize any proper nouns (names of people or places)?

_____ 3. Did I place correct punctuation at the end of each sentence?

_____ 4. Did I indent my paragraph(s)?

_____ 5. Did I spell all words correctly, and did I use a dictionary to check the spelling of any words I was unsure about?

Holiday Description *(cont.)*

Publishing and Technology Option: Design a greeting card for your favorite holiday. On the outside of the card, draw a picture that represents the holiday. On the inside, write your description of the holiday. You could use a computer program to design your greeting card if you prefer. You might even choose to send the card to a special person.

Home-School Connection: Take a survey of your family members, asking each of them which holiday is their favorite. Be sure to have family members tell you why the holidays they specify are their favorites.

I can feel the excitement in the air as soon as I wake up. I have been waiting for this day all year. It is Christmas morning! I quietly lie in bed for a moment, trying to decide if it is too early to wake up my parents. I know that I will not be able to open any of my presents until my parents announce that it is time to come to the tree. I can hear my brothers and sisters whispering in the hallway. We go into my parents' room together, pouncing on their bed and screaming, "It's Christmas! It's Christmas!" We go downstairs and are amazed by brightly colored packages that surround the sweet smelling pine tree. After we tear into some presents, we have our traditional breakfast: sausage and egg casserole, cinnamon rolls, and hot chocolate. One of my brothers licks his lips when he smells the casserole. I smile at him, also imagining the taste of the holiday treats.

Holiday Description *(cont.)*

Assessment Rubric:

- Criteria for **EXCELLENT** holiday descriptions

_____ The description is written in a well-developed paragraph, with cohesive topic, detail, and concluding sentences.

_____ The description evokes strong sensory images.

_____ The author uses precise word choices to depict the subject of the description.

_____ The author uses many sophisticated sentence structures to enhance the description.

(Check all those included.)

❏ colon sentences   ❏ appositives   ❏ commas in a series
❏ semicolon sentences   ❏ transitions
❏ other: _____

_____ The author uses many effective writing techniques to enhance the description.

_____ Spelling, capitalization, and punctuation are correct.

- Criteria for **SATISFACTORY** holiday descriptions

_____ The description is written in a well-developed paragraph, with topic, detail, and concluding sentences.

_____ The description evokes sensory images.

_____ The author uses effective word choices to depict the subject of the description.

_____ The author uses some sophisticated sentence structures in the description.

(Check all those included.)

❏ colon sentences   ❏ appositives   ❏ commas in a series
❏ semicolon sentences   ❏ transitions
❏ other: _____

_____ The author uses some effective writing techniques to enhance the description.

_____ Spelling, capitalization, and punctuation errors do not interfere with the meaning of the description.

- Criteria for **UNSATISFACTORY** holiday descriptions

_____ The description may not be written in paragraph form and may lack topic, detail, and/or concluding sentences.

_____ The description does not include sensory images.

_____ The author does not use effective word choices to depict the subject of the description.

_____ The author does not use sophisticated sentence structures in the description.

_____ The author does not use effective writing techniques to enhance the description.

_____ Spelling, capitalization, and punctuation errors interfere with the meaning of the description.

Menu Rewrite

Descriptive Writing Assignment: Take a look at the menu of your school cafeteria. Notice what is being served for lunch and the way the menu is presented. Think about your experiences eating in the school cafeteria. Decide whether you liked or disliked the food.

Rewrite the school cafeteria menu, using specific words to either make the food sound delicious or horrible. You may wish to consult several restaurant menus to get ideas for how they make the food sound good to eat. Use your knowledge of the connotations of words to help with your description. Write your new menu in paragraph form. Be sure to include specific details, using precise word choices. Try to use sophisticated sentence structures and effective writing techniques, as appropriate. Before creating a final draft, revise and proofread your work using the checklists provided below.

Revising: When you have completed your rough draft, revise your description using the following checklist of questions.

_____ 1. Did I use the best possible word choices to describe my subject?

_____ 2. Did I use sophisticated sentence structures to enhance my description?

(colon sentences, semicolon sentences, commas in a series, appositives, transitions, etc.)

_____ 3. Did I use effective writing techniques to enhance my description?

(similes, metaphors, onomatopoeia, hyperbole, etc.)

_____ 4. Did I include a topic sentence, detail sentences, and a concluding sentence?

_____ 5. Do my descriptions give the impression I want?

Proofreading: Before you write your final draft, proofread your description using the following checklist of questions.

_____ 1. Did I capitalize the first word of each sentence?

_____ 2. Did I capitalize any proper nouns (names of people or places)?

_____ 3. Did I place correct punctuation at the end of each sentence?

_____ 4. Did I indent my paragraph(s)?

_____ 5. Did I spell all words correctly, and did I use a dictionary to check the spelling of any words I was unsure about?

Menu Rewrite *(cont.)*

Publishing and Technology Option: Design a menu cover for your school cafeteria. Create a logo and illustrate the menu. You could draw the logo by hand or use a drawing or graphics program on a computer. Write or type your description of the meal on the inside of the menu.

Home-School Connection: Describe your dinner in a positive manner.

Today's lunch will feature a variety of interesting items that will tempt your tummy. The main item on the menu is Sloppy Joe sandwiches, the messiest food around. Comprised of overcooked mystery meat slathered in mounds of ketchup, Sloppy Joe sandwiches are sure to be a smashing success. For those who do not care for the soggy roll that will fall apart as soon as you bite into the sandwich, we have provided some hard, stale rolls. Contact the nurse about any broken teeth. There is, of course, a creative vegetable side dish to accompany the Sloppy Joe sandwiches. Stringy green beans that have been sitting in cans for approximately five years should satisfy even the most ravenous student. For those students who would like to incorporate additional vegetables into their lunch, we will be rolling out the salad cart today. If some of the items look the same as last week, it's because they are the same. Waste not, want not is our school cafeteria's policy. Any mold can be easily scraped off of the pasta or potato salads. In an effort to ensure that students consume enough protein, we have left the worms in the tomatoes and lettuce. Tapioca is the last item we will be serving. If you crunch something in your tapioca pudding, just swallow it. You probably don't want to know how we make it. If anyone is still hungry after eating all of these items, they need only come to the kitchen and request additional food. We have a number of leftovers, some from the first week of school. We hope that you will all enjoy this nourishing, satisfying lunch.

Menu Rewrite *(cont.)*

Assessment Rubric:

- Criteria for **EXCELLENT** menu rewrites

_____ The description is written in a well-developed paragraph, with cohesive topic, detail, and concluding sentences.

_____ The description evokes strong sensory images.

_____ The author uses precise word choices to depict the subject of the description.

_____ The author uses many sophisticated sentence structures to enhance the description.

(Check all those included.)

❏ colon sentences ❏ appositives ❏ commas in a series
❏ semicolon sentences ❏ transitions
❏ other: _____

_____ The author uses many effective writing techniques to enhance the description.

_____ Spelling, capitalization, and punctuation are correct.

- Criteria for **SATISFACTORY** menu rewrites

_____ The description is written in a well-developed paragraph, with topic, detail, and concluding sentences.

_____ The description evokes sensory images.

_____ The author uses effective word choices to depict the subject of the description.

_____ The author uses some sophisticated sentence structures in the description.

(Check all those included.)

❏ colon sentences ❏ appositives ❏ commas in a series
❏ semicolon sentences ❏ transitions
❏ other: _____

_____ The author uses some effective writing techniques to enhance the description.

_____ Spelling, capitalization, and punctuation errors do not interfere with the meaning of the description.

- Criteria for **UNSATISFACTORY** menu rewrites

_____ The description may not be written in paragraph form and may lack topic, detail, and/or concluding sentences.

_____ The description does not include sensory images.

_____ The author does not use effective word choices to depict the subject of the description.

_____ The author does not use sophisticated sentence structures in the description.

_____ The author does not use effective writing techniques to enhance the description.

_____ Spelling, capitalization, and punctuation errors interfere with the meaning of the description.

Monster Description

Descriptive Writing Assignment: Create a monster. Use crayons, markers, colored pencils—anything you like to draw a picture of a monster. When you finish, think about what your monster looks like, its facial features, the color of its skin, the size and shape of its body, and how it moves.

Write a paragraph describing the appearance of your monster. Be sure to include specific details, using precise word choices. Try to use sophisticated sentence structures and effective writing techniques, as appropriate. Before creating a final draft, revise and proofread your work using the checklists provided below.

Revising: When you have completed your rough draft, revise your description using the following checklist of questions.

_____ 1. Did I use the best possible word choices to describe my subject?

_____ 2. Did I use sophisticated sentence structures to enhance my description?

(colon sentences, semicolon sentences, commas in a series, appositives, transitions, etc.)

_____ 3. Did I use effective writing techniques to enhance my description?

(similes, metaphors, onomatopoeia, hyperbole, etc.)

_____ 4. Did I include a topic sentence, detail sentences, and a concluding sentence?

_____ 5. Does my description allow the reader to "see" the monster?

Proofreading: Before you write your final draft, proofread your description using the following checklist of questions.

_____ 1. Did I capitalize the first word of each sentence?

_____ 2. Did I capitalize any proper nouns (names of people or places)?

_____ 3. Did I place correct punctuation at the end of each sentence?

_____ 4. Did I indent my paragraph(s)?

_____ 5. Did I spell all words correctly, and did I use a dictionary to check the spelling of any words I was unsure about?

Monster Description *(cont.)*

Publishing and Technology Option: Create a frame for your monster picture. Heavy cardboard or poster board works well. Make it a double frame and put your picture on one side and your description of your monster on the other side. Use a word-processing program on a computer to type your monster description.

Home-School Connection: Have a family member read your monster description and try to draw your monster. Don't help. If your writing is clear and precise, your family member's monster will look very much like the one you imagined.

Harry, the scary monster, is not someone you want to encounter on a dark night. Unlike anyone you have ever seen, Harry has an octagonal face. There are short, purple spikes of hair sticking out from all around his head, making his head look like a purple sun. His green nose resembles a long, thin triangle that points down toward his mouth. His blue-tinged lips are cracked on either side of his mouth. There is a large white sore on his top lip. His lips are parted, revealing four rows—two on the top and two on the bottom—of dagger-sharp teeth. The teeth are a dingy yellow color, scarred with mud-brown spots. On either side of his nose lie Harry's triangular, orange ears. Dirty clumps of ear wax hang on the coarse bristles of hair that stick out of each ear. The hair is brittle and disgusting, comparable only to the strands of brown hair that emerge from Harry's chin. Harry's beard is tangled in his curly green chest hair, which covers his mottled skin. The eight legs that grow out of his chest are hairless, revealing white skin with bright red spots. Blue veins are clearly visible through Harry's see-through skin. At the bottom of his legs lie his strange, bird-like, turquoise feet. He has only three toes, each with a long, sharp claw at the end. Harry walks on just two of his eight legs. His long, scaly, green tail is often used for additional support. When he is standing at rest, Harry leans on his green tail to relax. His tail can also be used as a weapon if Harry feels threatened. You do not want to threaten Harry. In fact you do not want to be anywhere near Harry. Now that you know exactly what Harry looks like, you should be able to avoid him.

Monster Description *(cont.)*

Assessment Rubric:

- Criteria for **EXCELLENT** monster descriptions

_____ The description is written in a well-developed paragraph, with cohesive topic, detail, and concluding sentences.

_____ The description evokes strong sensory images.

_____ The author uses precise word choices to depict the subject of the description.

_____ The author uses many sophisticated sentence structures to enhance the description.

(Check all those included.)

❑ colon sentences   ❑ appositives   ❑ commas in a series
❑ semicolon sentences   ❑ transitions
❑ other: _____

_____ The author uses many effective writing techniques to enhance the description.

_____ Spelling, capitalization, and punctuation are correct.

- Criteria for **SATISFACTORY** monster descriptions

_____ The description is written in a well-developed paragraph, with topic, detail, and concluding sentences.

_____ The description evokes sensory images.

_____ The author uses effective word choices to depict the subject of the description.

_____ The author uses some sophisticated sentence structures in the description.

(Check all those included.)

❑ colon sentences   ❑ appositives   ❑ commas in a series
❑ semicolon sentences   ❑ transitions
❑ other: _____

_____ The author uses some effective writing techniques to enhance the description.

_____ Spelling, capitalization, and punctuation errors do not interfere with the meaning of the description.

- Criteria for **UNSATISFACTORY** monster descriptions

_____ The description may not be written in paragraph form and may lack topic, detail, and/or concluding sentences.

_____ The description does not include sensory images.

_____ The author does not use effective word choices to depict the subject of the description.

_____ The author does not use sophisticated sentence structures in the description.

_____ The author does not use effective writing techniques to enhance the description.

_____ Spelling, capitalization, and punctuation errors interfere with the meaning of the description.

Room Description

Descriptive Writing Assignment: Look around your room. Think about the following: the furniture in your room, the toys in your room, any decorations in your room, the colors in your room, and what other people say about your room.

Write a paragraph describing the appearance of your room. Be sure to include details, using precise word choices. Try to use sophisticated sentence structures and effective writing techniques, as appropriate. Before creating a final draft, revise and proofread your work using the checklists provided below.

Revising: When you have completed your rough draft, revise your description using the following checklist of questions.

_____ 1. Did I use the best possible word choices to describe my subject?

_____ 2. Did I use sophisticated sentence structures to enhance my description?

(colon sentences, semicolon sentences, commas in a series, appositives, transitions, etc.)

_____ 3. Did I use effective writing techniques to enhance my description?

(similes, metaphors, onomatopoeia, hyperbole, etc.)

_____ 4. Did I include a topic sentence, detail sentences, and a concluding sentence?

_____ 5. Does my description allow the reader to "see" my room?

Proofreading: Before you write your final draft, proofread your description using the following checklist of questions.

_____ 1. Did I capitalize the first word of each sentence?

_____ 2. Did I capitalize any proper nouns (names of people or places)?

_____ 3. Did I place correct punctuation at the end of each sentence?

_____ 4. Did I indent my paragraph(s)?

_____ 5. Did I spell all words correctly, and did I use a dictionary to check the spelling of any words I was unsure about?

Room Description *(cont.)*

Publishing and Technology Option: Draw a diagram of your room. You could draw it freehand or use a drawing program on a computer. Be sure to include as much of the furniture and decorations as possible. Write your description on the back of your diagram.

Home-School Connection: Have a family member write a description of your room, and see how it compares to your description.

My mom says my room looks like a bomb went off in it. I don't really know what she means by that. I think it's a cool room; it's got everything a kid could want. When you walk into my room, you'll see posters all over the walls. I like sports, and there is a poster from every sport I like: football, baseball, soccer, lacrosse, and ice hockey. I also have pictures on the walls that I drew. I like to draw aliens and science fiction things. My bed is on the right side of my room. I have an awesome bed; the bedposts are shaped like baseball bats! My comforter is navy blue and my sheets are light blue. You would see that if you walked in my room because I never make my bed. I take my school clothes off before I go outside to play, and I throw them on the floor. If there weren't so many clothes on the floor, you could see my tan carpeting. Right beside my bed, there is a dark brown stain on the carpet. I spilled soda there once. My furniture is wooden. I have a dresser along the left wall. It has a mirror on it. Beside my bed, I have a nightstand with a football lamp on it. I have a navy blue beanbag chair in the back corner of my bedroom. Across from my bed, I have my entertainment paradise: my radio, my television, and my games.

Room Description *(cont.)*

Assessment Rubric:

- Criteria for **EXCELLENT** room descriptions

_____ The description is written in a well-developed paragraph, with cohesive topic, detail, and concluding sentences.

_____ The description evokes strong sensory images.

_____ The author uses precise word choices to depict the subject of the description.

_____ The author uses many sophisticated sentence structures to enhance the description.

(Check all those included.)

❏ colon sentences   ❏ appositives   ❏ commas in a series
❏ semicolon sentences   ❏ transitions
❏ other: _____

_____ The author uses many effective writing techniques to enhance the description.

_____ Spelling, capitalization, and punctuation are correct.

- Criteria for **SATISFACTORY** room descriptions

_____ The description is written in a well-developed paragraph, with topic, detail, and concluding sentences.

_____ The description evokes sensory images.

_____ The author uses effective word choices to depict the subject of the description.

_____ The author uses some sophisticated sentence structures in the description.

(Check all those included.)

❏ colon sentences   ❏ appositives   ❏ commas in a series
❏ semicolon sentences   ❏ transitions
❏ other: _____

_____ The author uses some effective writing techniques to enhance the description.

_____ Spelling, capitalization, and punctuation errors do not interfere with the meaning of the description.

- Criteria for **UNSATISFACTORY** room descriptions

_____ The description may not be written in paragraph form and may lack topic, detail, and/or concluding sentences.

_____ The description does not include sensory images.

_____ The author does not use effective word choices to depict the subject of the description.

_____ The author does not use sophisticated sentence structures in the description.

_____ The author does not use effective writing techniques to enhance the description.

_____ Spelling, capitalization, and punctuation errors interfere with the meaning of the description.

Runway Model Description

Descriptive Writing Assignment: Notice the outfit that a friend or relative is wearing. Pretend that this person is a fashion model, strolling down the runway, modeling his or her outfit. Think about the articles of clothing the person is wearing. Notice the following: the fabrics and textures of the clothes, the shades of color in the clothing, and how the pieces of clothing "work" together to create the outfit.

Write a paragraph describing your friend or relative's outfit, as though that person was a fashion model. Be sure to include specific details, using precise word choices. Try to use sophisticated sentence structures and effective writing techniques, as appropriate. Before creating a final draft, revise and proofread your work using the checklists provided below.

Revising: When you have completed your rough draft, revise your description using the following checklist of questions.

_____   1. Did I use the best possible word choices to describe my subject?

_____   2. Did I use sophisticated sentence structures to enhance my description?

(colon sentences, semicolon sentences, commas in a series, appositives, transitions, etc.)

_____   3. Did I use effective writing techniques to enhance my description?

(similes, metaphors, onomatopoeia, hyperbole, etc.)

_____   4. Did I include a topic sentence, detail sentences, and a concluding sentence?

_____   5. Will my description allow the reader to "see" the outfit?

Proofreading: Before you write your final draft, proofread your description using the following checklist of questions.

_____   1. Did I capitalize the first word of each sentence?

_____   2. Did I capitalize any proper nouns (names of people or places)?

_____   3. Did I place correct punctuation at the end of each sentence?

_____   4. Did I indent my paragraph(s)?

_____   5. Did I spell all words correctly, and did I use a dictionary to check the spelling of any words I was unsure about?

Runway Model Description *(cont.)*

Publishing and Technology Option: Use a digital camera to take a picture of your subject, modeling the outfit. Export the picture to your word processed final draft. Print the picture with your description. If you do not have access to a digital camera, take a picture with a regular camera and scan in the image. Another option is to draw a picture of your subject using a drawing program on a computer.

Home-School Connection: Have a family fashion show. Have every member of your family dress in his or her favorite outfit. Create a "runway" in a hallway or family room. Describe your family members' outfits as they stroll down the "runway."

Susie's casual outfit shows off her slim, athletic figure. Her white cotton shirt is simple and elegant. A pale yellow heart draws attention to the shirt. The heart is a shiny, silky material in very pale yellow. The collar and short sleeves of the shirt are trimmed with thin, blue lace. Her jeans accent the blue lace on her shirt. Susie's denim jeans are a light shade of blue with streaks of white throughout each leg. The buttons are a shiny, brass color, adding a touch of elegance to her outfit. Her brown leather belt has a matching shiny, brass buckle, in a big "S" shape. The belt is too long for Susie's waist, so she wears it wrapped twice around her body. Susie's knee-high boots are unique. The smooth, black leather boots feature a purple velvet edge around the top of each boot. Susie's outfit is well-coordinated from head to toe. Her long, flowing hair is secured by a purple velvet headband that exactly matches the purple velvet trim around her boots. Purple ribbons stream down from the headband, swirling through her jet-black hair. Susie's tiny, brass earrings are ringed with circles of purple velvet. Thin, brass chains hang down from the earrings, creating a beautiful, musical sound when they clink together. Susie's ensemble is beautiful and versatile, perfect for a day at school or an evening at the mall.

Runway Model Description *(cont.)*

Assessment Rubric:

- Criteria for **EXCELLENT** runway model descriptions

_____ The description is written in a well-developed paragraph, with cohesive topic, detail, and concluding sentences.

_____ The description evokes strong sensory images.

_____ The author uses precise word choices to depict the subject of the description.

_____ The author uses many sophisticated sentence structures to enhance the description.

(Check all those included.)

❏ colon sentences   ❏ appositives   ❏ commas in a series
❏ semicolon sentences   ❏ transitions
❏ other: _____

_____ The author uses many effective writing techniques to enhance the description.

_____ Spelling, capitalization, and punctuation are correct.

- Criteria for **SATISFACTORY** runway model descriptions

_____ The description is written in a well-developed paragraph, with topic, detail, and concluding sentences.

_____ The description evokes sensory images.

_____ The author uses effective word choices to depict the subject of the description.

_____ The author uses some sophisticated sentence structures in the description.

(Check all those included.)

❏ colon sentences   ❏ appositives   ❏ commas in a series
❏ semicolon sentences   ❏ transitions
❏ other: _____

_____ The author uses some effective writing techniques to enhance the description.

_____ Spelling, capitalization, and punctuation errors do not interfere with the meaning of the description.

- Criteria for **UNSATISFACTORY** runway model descriptions

_____ The description may not be written in paragraph form and may lack topic, detail, and/or concluding sentences.

_____ The description does not include sensory images.

_____ The author does not use effective word choices to depict the subject of the description.

_____ The author does not use sophisticated sentence structures in the description.

_____ The author does not use effective writing techniques to enhance the description.

_____ Spelling, capitalization, and punctuation errors interfere with the meaning of the description.

Shoe Description

Descriptive Writing Assignment: Take off one of your shoes and study it carefully. Think about the following: the style of your shoe, the size and shape of your shoe, the color(s) of your shoe, and the function of your shoe.

Write a paragraph describing the appearance of your shoe. Be sure to include specific details, using precise word choices. Try to use sophisticated sentence structures and effective writing techniques, as appropriate. Before creating a final draft, revise and proofread your work using the checklists provided below.

Revising: When you have completed your rough draft, revise your description using the following checklist of questions.

_____ 1. Did I use the best possible word choices to describe my subject?

_____ 2. Did I use sophisticated sentence structures to enhance my description?

      (colon sentences, semicolon sentences, commas in a series, appositives, transitions, etc.)

_____ 3. Did I use effective writing techniques to enhance my description?

      (similes, metaphors, onomatopoeia, hyperbole, etc.)

_____ 4. Did I include a topic sentence, detail sentences, and a concluding sentence?

_____ 5. Does my description allow the reader to "see" my shoe?

Proofreading: Before you write your final draft, proofread your description using the following checklist of questions.

_____ 1. Did I capitalize the first word of each sentence?

_____ 2. Did I capitalize any proper nouns (names of people or places)?

_____ 3. Did I place correct punctuation at the end of each sentence?

_____ 4. Did I indent my paragraph(s)?

_____ 5. Did I spell all words correctly, and did I use a dictionary to check the spelling of any words I was unsure about?

Shoe Description *(cont.)*

Publishing and Technology Option: Use a digital camera to take a picture of your shoe. Print the picture to create an illustration for your description. As an alternative, use a computer drawing program to draw a picture of your shoe. Then print the picture to go with your description.

Home-School Connection: Line up all of your shoes. Read your description to a family member and see if that person can determine which shoe you are describing.

The boot is tall, reaching halfway up my leg when I pull it on. It is made of chestnut brown leather. The soft, cocoa brown fur that lines the inside and borders the top of the boot keeps my foot and leg warm. The boot is so warm that I cannot wear it for very long if I am inside. The thick, brown and gray laces are laced through eight metal rings on the boot. The thick sole and one-inch (2.5 cm) heel on the boot add two inches (5 cm) to my height, making me taller when I wear these boots. The tread on the bottom of the boot is more than an inch (2.5 cm) thick. Around the outside of the sole, the tread looks much like a tire and seems just as effective when it comes to gripping the snow or ice. Down the center of the sole, the tread is made up of a series of three dimensional stars. This design creates a beautiful footprint in the snow. The sole is sewed onto the boot with long white stitches. The tread at the front of the boot is slightly worn down. The toe of the boot is scuffed and worn from dragging my feet when I go sledding. The brown leather is scratched and peeling on parts of the toe. These are my favorite boots because I wear them on snowy days when we don't have school.

Shoe Description *(cont.)*

Assessment Rubric:

- Criteria for **EXCELLENT** shoe descriptions

_____ The description is written in a well-developed paragraph, with cohesive topic, detail, and concluding sentences.

_____ The description evokes strong sensory images.

_____ The author uses precise word choices to depict the subject of the description.

_____ The author uses many sophisticated sentence structures to enhance the description.

(Check all those included.)

❑ colon sentences   ❑ appositives   ❑ commas in a series

❑ semicolon sentences   ❑ transitions

❑ other: _____

_____ The author uses many effective writing techniques to enhance the description.

_____ Spelling, capitalization, and punctuation are correct.

- Criteria for **SATISFACTORY** shoe descriptions

_____ The description is written in a well-developed paragraph, with topic, detail, and concluding sentences.

_____ The description evokes sensory images.

_____ The author uses effective word choices to depict the subject of the description.

_____ The author uses some sophisticated sentence structures in the description.

(Check all those included.)

❑ colon sentences   ❑ appositives   ❑ commas in a series

❑ semicolon sentences   ❑ transitions

❑ other: _____

_____ The author uses some effective writing techniques to enhance the description.

_____ Spelling, capitalization, and punctuation errors do not interfere with the meaning of the description.

- Criteria for **UNSATISFACTORY** shoe descriptions

_____ The description may not be written in paragraph form and may lack topic, detail, and/or concluding sentences.

_____ The description does not include sensory images.

_____ The author does not use effective word choices to depict the subject of the description.

_____ The author does not use sophisticated sentence structures in the description.

_____ The author does not use effective writing techniques to enhance the description.

_____ Spelling, capitalization, and punctuation errors interfere with the meaning of the description.

Animal Description

Descriptive Writing Assignment: Hold your favorite teddy bear, stuffed animal, or pet. Look closely at the animal. Think about the following: how it feels to hold the animal, what its texture is like, what color it is, what its features look like, what its size and shape are, what it smells like, and what the animal means to you.

Write a paragraph describing your favorite teddy bear, stuffed animal, or pet. Be sure to include specific details, using precise word choices. Try to use sophisticated sentence structures and effective writing techniques, as appropriate. Before creating a final draft, revise and proofread your work using the checklists provided below.

Revising: When you have completed your rough draft, revise your description using the following checklist of questions.

_____ 1. Did I use the best possible word choices to describe my subject?

_____ 2. Did I use sophisticated sentence, structures to enhance my description?

(colon sentences, semicolon sentences, commas in a series, appositives, transitions, etc.)

_____ 3. Did I use effective writing techniques to enhance my description?

(similes, metaphors, onomatopoeia, hyperbole, etc.)

_____ 4. Did I include a topic sentence, detail sentences, and a concluding sentence?

_____ 5. Does my description allow the reader to "experience" my favorite teddy bear, stuffed animal or pet?

Proofreading: Before you write your final draft, proofread your description using the following checklist of questions.

_____ 1. Did I capitalize the first word of each sentence?

_____ 2. Did I capitalize any proper nouns (names of people or places)?

_____ 3. Did I place correct punctuation at the end of each sentence?

_____ 4. Did I indent my paragraph(s)?

_____ 5. Did I spell all words correctly, and did I use a dictionary to check the spelling of any words I was unsure about?

Animal Description *(cont.)*

Publishing and Technology Option: Create a pawprint border around your description.

Home-School Connection: Ask a family member to take you to the local zoo. Find an interesting animal. Talk with your family member about how you would describe that animal.

CC is a sleek, charcoal gray cat whose shiny coat glimmers in the sunshine. His body is long and lean, even when it is curled in a ball on my lap. He is a medium-sized cat, no bigger than my Dad's shoe. His nose is soft and velvety to the touch. His pink, pointed ears hear every sound, even when he is relaxed. His tail is tall and bushy, sticking straight up in the air when he gets excited. My grandmother is allergic to CC. She says he smells "fuzzy." I think he smells like cat food. My favorite time with CC is when he curls up in my lap and I pet him.

Animal Description *(cont.)*

Assessment Rubric:

- Criteria for **EXCELLENT** animal descriptions

_____ The description is written in a well-developed paragraph, with cohesive topic, detail, and concluding sentences.

_____ The description evokes strong sensory images.

_____ The author uses precise word choices to depict the subject of the description.

_____ The author uses many sophisticated sentence structures to enhance the description.

(Check all those included.)

❑ colon sentences ❑ appositives ❑ commas in a series
❑ semicolon sentences ❑ transitions
❑ other: _____

_____ The author uses many effective writing techniques to enhance the description.

_____ Spelling, capitalization, and punctuation are correct.

- Criteria for **SATISFACTORY** animal descriptions

_____ The description is written in a well-developed paragraph, with topic, detail, and concluding sentences.

_____ The description evokes sensory images.

_____ The author uses effective word choices to depict the subject of the description.

_____ The author uses some sophisticated sentence structures in the description.

(Check all those included.)

❑ colon sentences ❑ appositives ❑ commas in a series
❑ semicolon sentences ❑ transitions
❑ other: _____

_____ The author uses some effective writing techniques to enhance the description.

_____ Spelling, capitalization, and punctuation errors do not interfere with the meaning of the description.

- Criteria for **UNSATISFACTORY** animal descriptions

_____ The description may not be written in paragraph form and may lack topic, detail, and/or concluding sentences.

_____ The description does not include sensory images.

_____ The author does not use effective word choices to depict the subject of the description.

_____ The author does not use sophisticated sentence structures in the description.

_____ The author does not use effective writing techniques to enhance the description.

_____ Spelling, capitalization, and punctuation errors interfere with the meaning of the description.

Vacation Spot Description

Descriptive Writing Assignment: Pick your favorite vacation spot. Think about the following: its temperature, its geographical features, the colors you see in this place, what you like to do in this vacation spot, and how you feel when you are in this place.

Write a paragraph describing your favorite vacation spot. Be sure to include specific details, using precise word choices. Try to use sophisticated sentence structures and effective writing techniques, as appropriate. Before creating a final draft, revise and proofread your work using the checklists provided below.

Revising: When you have completed your rough draft, revise your description using the following checklist of questions.

_____   1. Did I use the best possible word choices to describe my subject?

_____   2. Did I use sophisticated sentence structures to enhance my description?

                (colon sentences, semicolon sentences, commas in a series, appositives, sentence, transitions, etc.)

_____   3. Did I use effective writing techniques to enhance my description?

                (similes, metaphors, onomatopoeia, hyperbole, etc.)

_____   4. Did I include a topic sentence, detail sentences, and a concluding sentence?

_____   5. Does my description allow the reader to "experience" my this vaction spot?

Proofreading: Before you write your final draft, proofread your description using the following checklist of questions.

_____   1. Did I capitalize the first word of each sentence?

_____   2. Did I capitalize any proper nouns (names of people or places)?

_____   3. Did I place correct punctuation at the end of each sentence?

_____   4. Did I indent my paragraph(s)?

_____   5. Did I spell all words correctly, and did I use a dictionary to check the spelling of any words I was unsure about?

Vacation Spot Description *(cont.)*

Publishing and Technology Options: Create a travel brochure for you favorite vacation spot. Include illustrations and your description in your brochure. Try to entice other people to visit your favorite spot.

Home-School Connection: Talk with a family member about the places you have visited. Compare several places. Describe the locations and features of each place. Discuss the differences and similarities among the various vacation spots.

Hot, streaming sunlight glistens off the warm aquamarine waters as the tan sandy beach fills with the sounds of frolicking children on a warm, summer afternoon. Two teenagers flying a kite on the far end of the beach release the string, letting the kite fly high above the sand. In the distance, a volleyball net is barely visible. It is surrounded by vacationers running and jumping to hit a large white ball. The beach is dotted with bright, colorful umbrellas sheltering families from the hot, midday sun. The air is scented with the sweet coconut oil that people slather on their exposed backs. One woman plays some quiet music on the radio. Another woman smiles contentedly, breathing in a mouthful of fresh, salty, sea air. The lifeguard, high in the white, wooden chair keeps a careful watch on the children playing in the surf. His skin, like the skin of many on the beach, is tanned to a deep, golden color. Before his chair lies a bright red buoy, a reminder of the danger that lies behind the beauty of the surf. His eyes move constantly, scanning the water, particularly just to the right of his chair. The jetty is a long walk down the beach, but he has seen children pulled quickly into the line of sharp, mossy rocks. His shrill whistle is heard often throughout the day as he warns swimmers to retreat from the harsh jetty. The lifeguard is the gatekeeper for this peaceful vacation spot, reminding families about the dangerous jetty.

Vacation Spot Description *(cont.)*

Assessment Rubric:

- Criteria for **EXCELLENT** vacation spot descriptions

_____ The description is written in a well-developed paragraph, with cohesive topic, detail, and concluding sentences.

_____ The description evokes strong sensory images.

_____ The author uses precise word choices to depict the subject of the description.

_____ The author uses many sophisticated sentence structures to enhance the description.

(Check all those included.)

❏ colon sentences   ❏ appositives   ❏ commas in a series
❏ semicolon sentences   ❏ transitions
❏ other: _____

_____ The author uses many effective writing techniques to enhance the description.

_____ Spelling, capitalization, and punctuation are correct.

- Criteria for **SATISFACTORY** vacation spot descriptions

_____ The description is written in a well-developed paragraph, with topic, detail, and concluding sentences.

_____ The description evokes sensory images.

_____ The author uses effective word choices to depict the subject of the description.

_____ The author uses some sophisticated sentence structures in the description.

(Check all those included.)

❏ colon sentences   ❏ appositives   ❏ commas in a series
❏ semicolon sentences   ❏ transitions
❏ other: _____

_____ The author uses some effective writing techniques to enhance the description.

_____ Spelling, capitalization, and punctuation errors do not interfere with the meaning of the description.

- Criteria for **UNSATISFACTORY** vacation spot descriptions

_____ The description may not be written in paragraph form and may lack topic, detail, and/or concluding sentences.

_____ The description does not include sensory images.

_____ The author does not use effective word choices to depict the subject of the description.

_____ The author does not use sophisticated sentence structures in the description.

_____ The author does not use effective writing techniques to enhance the description.

_____ Spelling, capitalization, and punctuation errors interfere with the meaning of the description.